INDRA-DHANUSA

An Annotated Bibliography of Indian Painting

(THROUGH THE AGES)

Prof. R. Nath

CONTENTS

ABBREVIATIONS

AI — Ancient India New Delhi, Nos. 1 (1945) to 22 (1966)

AIOC — All India Oriental Conference, Sessions I (Poona 1919) to XXII (Gauhati 1965)

AR — Asiatick Researches London/Calcutta, Vols. I (1788) to XX (1839) (Closed)

BH — 'Bharati' (Bulletin of the Department of Ancient Indian History Archaeology & Culture Banares Hindu University) Varanasi, Vols. 1 (1956) to 14 (1971)

BMB — Baroda Museum & Picture Gallery Bulletin Baroda, Vols. I (1943) to XXVII (1976-77)

BPOW — Bulletin of the Prince of Wales Museum of W. I. Bombay, Nos. 1 (1950-51) to 12 (1973) (Closed)

CHHAVI — 'Chhavi' Bharat Kala Bhawan Golden Jubilee Volume (1920-70) Bharat Kala Bhawan Varanasi (1971)

IAL — Indian Art & Letters London, Miscellaneous available volumes

IB — 'Indica' of the Heras Institute of Indian History & Culture Bombay, Vols. I (1964) to XVII (1980) and Silver Jubilee Commemoration Volume 1953

IC — Indian Culture Calcutta, Vols. I (1934) to XVI (1949)

IH — 'Itihas' of the Andhra Pradesh Archives, Hyderabad, Vols. I (1973) to VII (1979)

IHQ — Indian Historical Quarterly Calcutta, Vols. I (1925) to XXXIX (1963) (Closed)

II — 'Indo-Iranica' of the Iran Society Calcutta, Vols. I (1946) to XXXII (1979)

IMB — Indian Museum Bulletin Calcutta, Vols. I (1966) to XIII (1978)

IsC — Islamic Culture Hyderabad, Vols. I (1927) to LIV (1980)

JA — Jain Antiquary Arrah (Bihar), Vols. I (1935) to XXXII (1979)

JAS Journal of the Asiatic Society of Bengal Calcutta,
&
JASB —   I Series Vols. 1 (1832) to 75 (1904)
           II Series Vols. 1 (1905) to 30 (1934)
           III Series Vols. 1 (1935) to 19 (1953)
           IV Series Vols. 1 (1954) to 21 (1979)

JBORS — Journal of the Bihar & Orissa Research Society Patna, Vols. I (1915) onwards

JIA — Journal of Indian Art

JIH — Journal of Indian History Lucknow/Madras/Trivandrum, Vols. I (1922) to LVII (1979)

JISOA — Journal of the Indian Society of Oriental Art Calcutta,
           Old Series Vols. I (1933) to XIX (1952-53)
           Special Numbers 1961 and 1966
           New Series Vols. I (1965-66) to VIII (1976-77)
           and Dr Motichandra Commemoration Vol. (1978)

JJ — 'Jijñāsā' of the Department of Indian History & Culture University of Rajasthan Jaipur Vols. I (January 1974) to II. 1-2 (April 1975)

JJC — Jain Journal Calcutta, Vols. I (1966) to XV (1980)

JOI — Journal of the Oriental Institute Baroda, Vols. I (1951-52) to XXIX (June 1980)

JOR — Journal of Oriental Research of the K. S. R. Institute Madras, Vols. 1 (1927) to 39 (1969-70)

JPHS — Journal of the Panjab Historical Society Calcutta Vols. I (1911) to VIII (1921)... ...(Closed)

JSB — Jain Siddhanta Bhaskar Arrah (Bihar) (Hindi), Vols. I (1934) to XXXII (1979)

LK — 'Lalit Kala' of the Lalit Kala Akademi New Delhi, Nos. 1-2 (1955) to 19 (1979)

Marg — 'Marg' Bombay, Vols. I (1946-47) to XXXII (September 1979)

MB — 'Maru-Bharati' Pilani (Raj) (Hindi)

MG — 'Manisha' of the Gwalior Research Institute Gwalior Vol. I (1980)

MIAM — 'Medieval India : A Miscellany' of the Department of History, Aligarh Muslim University Aligarh, Vols. I (1969) to IV (1977)

NMB — National Museum Bulletin New Delhi, Nos. 1 to 3 (1972)

NPP — Nagari Pracharini Patrika Varanasi (Hindi), Vols. 1 to 82 (V. S. 2034/1977 A. D.)

MASB — Memoirs of the Asiatic Society of Bengal Calcutta, Vols. 1 to 12

PRHC — Proceedings of the Rajasthan History Congress (Raj), Vols. I (1967) to XI (1978)

PASB — Proceedings of the Asiatic Society of Bengal Calcutta

PP — 'Prachya-Pratibha' Bhopal, Vols. I (1973) to VII (1979)

QJNCPA — Quarterly Journal of the National Centre for the Performing Arts Bombay, Vols. I (1972) to IX (1980)

QRHS — Quarterly Review of Historical Studies Calcutta, Vols. I (1961-62) to XV (1975-76)

RAA — 'Rajput Art & Architecture' ed. by J. Jain and J. J. Neubauer (Wiesbaden, 1978) Collection of Hermann Goetz's articles on Rajput Art & Architecture

RB — 'Rajasthan Bharati' Bikaner (Hindi), Vols. I (1946) to XVIII (1976) (Closed)

RJ — 'Researcher' of the Department of Archaeology & Museums (Rajasthan) Jaipur, Nos. 1 (1961) to 13 (1973) (Closed)

viii

Dedication

This is dedicated to my second daughter Dr. Neelima Mittal (Ujjain) who drew its numerous sketches, designed it and worked extremely hard to prepare it artistically in accordance with the subject.

- Prof. R.Nath-

PREFACE

BIBLIOGRAPHY is not a clerical exercise. Without an intelligent Scheme which makes instant reference to the needed works possible; without a meaningful Selection of the Entries, including, of course, the learned Articles from standard Research-Journals; and without Annotations, it is not even worth the paper on which it is printed. It is easy to collect a few hundred catalogues, arrange the titles alphabetically and publish it subject-wise, all mechanically, without understanding the subject-matter. Instead of, and rather than, guiding into the right direction, such a compilation more misguides into confusion.

Thus :

I.   a **Plan and Scheme** of arrangement to ensure instant reference with the help of a series of accompanying indices;

II.   a useful **Selection** of entries; and

III.   **Annotations** giving the very necessary details of the region, the chronology and the subject of an entry,

are the three basic requirements of a BIBLIOGRAPHY.

One should, therefore, not only be well acquainted with the subject and the available literature uptodate, but he should also be thoroughly trained and experienced in Research which is a discipline in itself. This explains why such a great scholar of Muslim Art and Architecture as K. A. C. Creswell worked for nearly 45 years and produced a monumental 'BIBLIOGRAPHY OF ARCHITECTURE, ARTS AND CRAFTS OF ISLAM' (Cairo, 1961) in the evening of his life.

Much of our 'Research-scholars' time is consumed in finding the basic material of their research. The author remembers, while he was doing his Ph. D., when Prof. Sadhuram's Index to the **IHQ** had not been published, what was it like to stand by the recks in the narrow, semi-dark corridor of a Library and take out volumes of the Journal, one by one, read the contents and discover such wonderful articles as A. K. Coomaraswamy's 'SYMBOLISM OF THE DOME'. This went on for days and weeks together, in several libraries. Without bibliographies and indices, 50% **Research** comprised of the **Search of the Material.** The present work aspires to do this 50% work in this subject, i. e. to save the precious time of the scholars, art-historians and connoisseurs, provide them with the basic structure to begin with and facilitate their work.

A learned article of 10 pages is sometimes more informative and useful than a commercial book of 250 pages. Our elderly archaeologists, historians and scholars have been contributing valuable articles-comprising of the findings of their years of research-to journals. These articles constitute a monograph-of course, a mini-monograph-each. This tremendously useful material is lying concealed in the numerous journals beginning with the **Asiatick Researches,** Vol. I of which was published in 1788.

References to articles by such great savants as A. K. Coomaraswamy, Stella Kramrisch, O. C. Gangoly, Hermann Goetz, Motichandra, Rai Krishnadas, Karl J. Khandalavala, V. S Agarwal, Basil Gray, W. G. Archer, Doughlas Barrett, C. Sivaramamurti, U. P. Shah and others have been carefully collected. Articles from learned Research-journals of Indian Art (a select list whereof is given here-with) in English, Hindi and Gujarati have been selected for entries. French and German works are not, normally, accessible to the Indian scholar and, on account of this linguistic problem, these have not been included.

Some titles are self-indicative and need no annotations but, more often than not, only **annotations** make the entries in a Bibliography, as much as in an Index, intelligible and useful. For instance, the title of the article :

'Gu-Ge Bris : A Stylistic Amalgam'

is a riddle and its entry as such is of no use and meaningless in a Bibliography or Index without the following annotation :

"Painting style, extending from Lahul-Spiti to
Ladakh from 11th to 17th century, mainly Mural."

The present work also aspires to fill in the gaps in the study of Indian Painting : Mural, Miniature and Scroll, through the Ages. Chapter—1 entitled

'SANSKRIT TEXTS' contains entries on the **Theory of Indian Painting** which is a fundamental aspect of this study. Entries on 'GENERAL STUDIES IN INDIAN PAINTING' are given under Chapter-2. Chapter-3 on 'MURAL PAINTING' has been divided into two parts :

(A) dealing with **Ancient Indian Mural Paintings,** e. g. Ajanta, Bagh and Sittannavasal; and

(B) which deals with **Medieval Indian Mural Paintings** under such schools as Mughal, Rajput, Pahari and Deccani.

Chapter—4 is devoted to PAINTINGS ON PALM-LEAF AND CLOTH Chapter-5 contains entries on MINIATURE PAINTING. It is divided into several parts, each one devoted to a separate school, or two or three allied styles. Thus selected entries on **Buddhist, Nepalese and Eastern Indian Miniature Painting** are given in its Part (A). Part (B) bears the nomenclature 'Medieval Loka-Kala' which is not folk art. It is what we have been calling 'Jaina' and 'Apabhraṁsa' in the early stages and 'Rajasthani', 'Gujarati' and 'Western Indian' in the later. It is the school of indigenous styles of the medieval period from c. 11th century to roughly 17th century A. D., extending from Gujarat to Jaunpur, Malwa and the Deccan. (C) on 'Chinese Persian and Turkish Miniature Painting' has been included to give an understanding of an important source of Mughal Miniature Art. Entries on **Mughal** Miniature Painting, both 'Durbari' and 'Popular' have been given in Part (D); the so called 'Bazar' paintings have been read with the latter. To specific Theory of Medieval Painting, some Persian texts, e. g. The *Ain-i-Akbari* contain valuable references, these have also been included. Part (E) contains entries on the **'Rajput'** school consisting of such styles as Dhoondhar (Amer-Jaipur), Mewar, Bikaner, Jodhpur, Kishangarh, Bundi-Kota and others of medieval Rajasthan. Similarly popular nomenclature **'Pahari'** has been retained in Part (F) giving entries of Paintings of Kangra, Chamba, Guler, Basohli, Mankot, Nalagarh, Garhwal and other hill centres of Miniature art of Jammu-Kashmir, the Punjab, Himachal-Pradesh and Uttar Pradesh, including Painting under the Sikhs. (G) is on Miniature paintings of the **Deccan and South India**. A separate Chapter—6 has been devoted to the RAGA-MALA paintings of the Mughal, Rajput, Pahari and other schools. The last is Chapter—7 which contains a list of COMPANY AND BENGALI paintings of 19th and 20th centuries. Entries in this chapter are very selective for the simple reason that Modern Painting is still in the making and its theorisation (āstṛiya-karaṇa) has yet to begin, without which, i. e. without intellectualisation, mere practice is jejune. For details of Modern Indian Art and artists, reference may be made to the various publications, e. g. Lalit Kala Contemporary (Journal) Nos. 1-20, Prints (Multi-Colour reproductions), Folders, Portfolios and Books of the Lalit Kala Akademi New Delhi and various numbers of the Quarterly Journal Marg Bombay.

Some figures, e. g. of divinities, engraved on copper-plates and stone, also constitute an interesting study. The Gangola-tal Gwalior inscription of Mansingh Tomar contained a figure of Varāha. Some are preserved in the Mandu Museum. Many sites in Mewar, e. g. the Temple of Samādhiśvara at Chittorgarh, also have such figures. A few articles have been published on this subject but this data, at present, is not only very meagre but also so vague and inconsistent that a separate chapter on this topic could not be justified.

Though every effort has been made to cover the subject as comprehensively as possible, this is by no means exhaustive. In fact, it is a selective scheme and only really accessible, useful and important entries have been included. A few could have been left over. Supplements will follow.

The author is also aware that, in such a work as this, errors and omissions will always remain. For example, some casual references without page numbers have been included; these journals could not be available. In any case, it was deemed more useful to include them as they came to the view, than to drop them altogether. Srl No. 795 should have gone to 'Books' instead of being listed in 'Articles'; the error was detected when it was too late. Likewise, some entries missed the Serial and bear '—A' numbers in order of sequence.

The attempt is worthwhile, in any case, if it is deemed to be a good beginning and a step into the right direction.

Ajmer : 31 October 2018

Professor (Dr) R Nath,

M.A., Ph.D., D.Litt
(Retired Professor & Head of the Deptt
of History & Indian Culture, University of Rajasthan JAIPUR)
'Tapasya'
7, Gulab Bari Enclave
(Behind Asharam Chaudhary)
Gulab Bari
AJMER 305007 (Rajasthan, INDIA)

Mob 08278687716
profnath@gmail.com
www.rnath.in

1

SANSKRIT TEXTS
(Theory of Indian Painting)

BOOKS

BHATTACHARYA, A. K. 1
  'Chitra-Lakṣaṇa'
(Calcutta 1974)
Chapter on Painting from 16th century treatise on Indian Painting : Śrīkumāra's
'Śilpa-Ratna' ; it also deals with Mural Painting.

BHATTACHARYA, TARAPADA 2
  'Sculpture and Painting in Vāstuvidyā'
in **'The Canons of Indian Art'** *(Calcutta 1963) pp, 322-418.*
On the origin of Çitra and its texts; definition and classes, and other constituents
of Painting; a very learned enumeration. Its Appendix-H (pp. 426-38) deals with
colours and Vajralepa.

BHOJA, KING 3
  'Samarāṅgaṇa-Sūtradhāra'
*(ed. T. Ganapati Sastri and V. S. Agarwal, G. O. S. No. 25, Oriental
Institute Baroda 1966)*
Standard Mālava Śilpa text of the first half of the 11th century; its chapters 71-73
(pp. 582-90) and 79-82 (610-35) deal with Çitra and its various aspects. Its data
is translated and discussed by D. N. Shukla over and over again in several books,
e. g. **'Royal Arts'** (Lucknow 1967) Part—II, Çitra-Lakṣaṇam (Hindu Canons of
Painting) along with an outline History of Indian Painting, pp, 53-220; the same
Part—II, pp. 53-220 reproduced in **'Śilpa-Śāstra'** (Royal Palace & Royal Arts)
(Lucknow 1967); **'Yantra-Vijnāna evam Çitra Kalā'** (Hindi) (Lucknow 1967)
pp. 32-124 and Appendix pp.125-70; **'Vāstu-Śāstra'** Vol. II (Hindu Canons of
Iconography and Painting, Lucknow 1958).

BHUVANADEVĀCHĀRYA 4

'Aparājitapṛcchā'

(ed. P. A. Mankad, G. O. S. No. 115, Oriental Institute Baroda 1950).

Most standard- West Indian Śilpa text assignable to late 12th century A. D. Its chapters (Sūtṛas) 211 (p. 539), 224 (576-77), 227 (583-84), 231 (591) to 233 (595) deal with Çitṛa and its various aspects.Particularly useful is its chapter-224 on the definition of Çitṛa (which includes Painting and Sculpture).

BONER, ALICE 5

'Principles of Composition in Hindu Sculpture'

(Leiden 1962) pp. 260, 22 pls.

Its treatment of Form is equally applicable to Painting; reviewed in the **LK.** 11 (April 1962) 66-67.

CHATTERJEE, ASOKE SASTRI 6

'Viṣṇu-Dharmottara-Purāṇam' (Çitṛa-Sūtṛam)

(Varanasi 1971)

Text and Hindi tr. of 5 chapters (35-39) of the Çitṛa-Śūtṛa of III Khaṇḍa of the Viṣṇu-Dharmottara—Purāṇa with a scholarly Introduction in Sanskrit; **VDP** is a Khila of Viṣṇu—Purāṇa and its Third Khaṇḍa devoted to Fine Arts (Plastic and Performing) is assignable to c. 650 A.D.

COOMARASWAMY, ANANDA KENTISH 7

'(The) Transformation of Nature in Art'

(Dover, New York 1956)

On theories of Indian Art; the chapter on 'Ābhāsa' (pp.141-52) particularly deals with Painting; a very learned treatise of one of the greatest scholars of Indian Art.

DASGUPTA, S. N. 8

'Fundamentals of Indian Art'

(Bharatiya Vidya Bhawan Bombay 1969)

Deals mainly with the philosophy of Indian Art.

GANGOLY, O. C. 9

'Indian Art & Heritage'

(Calcutta 1957)

On the Aesthetics of Indian Painting and Sculpture.

GOSWAMY, B. N & DAHMEN-DALLAPICCOLA, A. L. 10

'(An) Early Document of Indian Art, the Chitṛalakṣaṇa of Nagnajit'

(Manohar, New Delhi 1976)

6th-7th century text on Painting and Sculpture; reviewed by Khandalavala in **LK** 19 (1979) 66.

KĀŚYAPA. MUNI 11

'Kāśyapa-Śilpam'
(ed. V. G. Apte, Anandashram Sanskrit Series No. 95 Poona 1926) also 'Kāśyapa-Śilpa-Śastṛa' *(Tanjore Saraswati Mahal Series No. 89, Tanjore 1960).*

South Indian Śilpa text assignable to c.1300 A. D. Its chapter-86 (pp. 257-59) deals with 'Varṇa—Lepana' or colour painting on Sculptures.

KRAMRISCH, STELLA (ed. & tr.) 12

'Viṣṇu-Dharmottara-Purāṇa'
(ed. and tr in English. Calcutta 1924)

First published text on Indian Painting, assignable to c.650 A. D. It corrects mistakes of the Venkateshwar edition but it has its own drawbacks.

MOTICHANDRA 13

'(The) Golden Flute'
(Lalit Kala Akademi, New Delhi 1962)

On the inter-relationship of Fine Arts particularly Indian Painting and Poetry.

NAGNAJIT 14

'Citra-Lakṣaṇa'
(Manohar, New Delhi 1976)

Tr. in English by B. N. Goswamy and Dahman-Dallapiccola, A.L., from its Tibetan version, under the title : 'An Early Document of Indian Art : The Chitralakṣaṇa of Nagnajit' (See No. 10 above).

SHAH, PRIYABALA (ed.) 15

'Viṣṇu-Dharmottara-Purāṇa' (3rd Khaṇḍa)
Vol. I (Sanskrit Text)
(ed. G. O. S. No. CXXX, Oriental Institute Baroda 1958)

Citra-Sūtra (Treatise on Painting) covers Chapters XXXV to XLIII, pp. 127-157 and deals with all related subjects; it is the earliest available text on Painting assignable to c. 650 A. D. the **VDP** is a Khila (Supplementary) of the Viṣṇu-Purāṇa.

SHAH, PRIYABALA 16

'Viṣṇu-Dharmottara-Purāṇa' (3rd Khaṇḍa)
Vol. II
(English rendering, with Introduction, Notes etc, G. O. S. No. 137, Oriental Institute Baroda 1961).

Citra-Sūtra is discussed pp. 98-137.

SHUKLA, D. N.   17

'Vāstu-Śāstra'

Vol. II (Hindu Canons of Iconography and Painting)
(*Lucknow 1958*).

A detailed enumeration of Indian Painting, mainly based on 'Samarāṅgaṇa-Sūtradhāra' of Bhoja of the first half of 11th century A. D. (See No. 3 above) with a historical and literary background; a very useful work for the study of Indian Painting.

SIVARAMAMURTI, C.   18

'Chitra–Sutra of the Vishnudharmottara'
(*New Delhi 1978*) *xiv+232, 141 pls.*

A very learned and authoritative discussion on the Çitṛa-Sūtṛa of the Viṣṇu-Dharmottara-Purāna of which text and English translation have also been given. It is the latest enumeration on the subject.

SOMEŚVARA, KING   19

'Mānasollāsa' (also called)
'Abhilāṣatārtha-Cintāmaṇi'
Vol. II

(ed. G. K. Shrigondekar, G. O. S. No. 84, Oriental Institute Baroda 1939, with English Introduction).

Pp. 13-18 deal with Painting and its various aspects. Of particular importance are its prescriptions on Mural Painting and preparation of colours. It was composed in 1131 A. D.

ŚRIKUMĀRA   20

'Śilpa–Ratnam'
Vol. I

(ed. T. Ganapati Sastri, Trivandrum Sanskrit Series No. 75 Trivandrum 1922).

16th century South Indian Śilpa text. Its 'Çitṛa-Lakṣaṇam' (pp. 244-58) deals with Çitṛa (Painting) and its various aspects in an abundantly useful way. This 'Çitṛa-Lakṣaṇam' has been tr. in English with critical notes by A. K. Bhattacharya in 'Chitra-Lakṣaṇa' (Calcutta 1974) (See No. 1 above). It also deals with Mural Painting authoritatively.

VARĀHAMIHIRA   21

'Bṛhat-Saṁhitā'
Part-II

(ed. A. V. Tripathi, Varanasi 1968).

5th-6th century text which also deals with Śilpa; its 56th chapter under the section on Temple Architecture (Prāsāda-Lakṣaṇa-Adhyāya) entitled 'Vajralepa' Lakṣaṇa' deals with Painting on the temple walls and sculptures.

ARTICLES

COOMARASWAMY, A. K. 29
'(The) Intellectual Operation in Indian Art'
JISOA, III (1935) 1-12

COOMARASWAMY, A. K. 30
'Onehundred References to Indian Painting'
AA, IV-1 (1930-32) 41-57 and 'Further References.' in AA, IV. 2-3, 126-29.
From the Upaniṣads, early and later Buddhist and Jaina literature, Epics, Sanskrit and Tamil Literature, inscriptions and other sources.

COOMARASWAMY, A. K. 31
•Viṣṇudharmottara'
(III. 41)
Journal of the American Oriental Society, Vol. 52 (1932)
Its Third Khaṇḍa deals with Fine Arts including Painting.

GHOSH, J. C. 32
'Nagnajit and the Antiquity of the Indian Art and Architecture'
IC, VI (1939-40) 347-51

JAYASWAL, K. P. 33
'A Hindu Text on Painting'
JBORS, IX (1923) 30-39

RAGHAVAN, V. 34
'Some Sanskrit Texts on Painting'
IHQ, IX-4 (1933) 898-911
Very important references.

RAGHAVAN, V. 35
'Two Chapters on Painting in the Nārada Śilpa Sāstṛa'
JISOA, III (1935) 15-32
An extremely important text on Indian Painting.

SIVARAMAMURTI, C. 36
'Antiquity and Evolution of Art in India'
JOR, VIII-4 (Oct-Dec 1934) 291-314; Part-II of the article published in the JOR, IX-1 (Jan-March 1935) 1-16.
A very learned study based on literary and other Sanskrit references on Indian Painting.

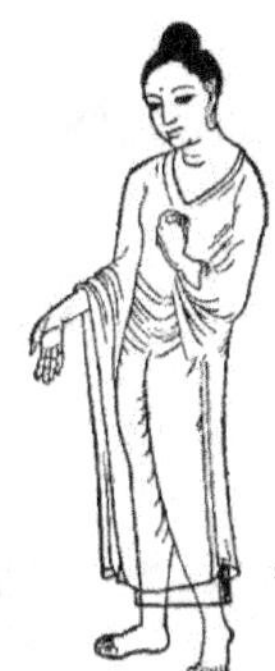

SIVARAMAMURTI, C.   37
    'A Passage on Painting from Nannechoḍa's Kumarasambhava'
MM. Kuppuswami Sastri Com. Vol. Madras (1935)

SIVARAMAMURTI, C.   38
    'A Passage on Painting in Potana's Bhagavata'
JOR, VI-2 (April–June 1932) 184–87
An Important text on Indian Painting.

SIVARAMAMURTI, C.   39
    '(The) Artist in Ancient India'
JOR, VIII-2 (April–June 1934) 168–99
A very learned monograph based on Ancient Indian literary and other references;
also see No. 111 below.

SIVARAMAMURTI, C.   40
    'Art Notes from Dhanapala's Tilaka-Manjari'
IC. Vol. II (1935–36) 199–210

SIVARAMAMURTI, C.   41
    'Citṛa-Śālās'
Triveni Madras, VII (1934)
Ancient Indian Art Galleries

SIVARAMAMURTI, C.   42
    'Conventions in the Art of Painting'
JOR, IX-3 (July–Sept 1935) 255–69
A very useful article based on Sanskrit literature.

SIVARAMAMURTI, C.   43
    'Fresco-Painting in the Śivatatva-Ratnākara'
Triveni Madras, V (1932)
Deals with its Theory.

SIVARAMAMURTI, C.   44
    'Realism in Indian Art'
JOR. IX-2 (April–June 1935) 100–118, 8 Figs
A very learned article based on Sanskrit literary references; mainly related to
Painting in Ancient India.

SIVARAMAMURTI, C.   45
    'Sanskrit Sayings based on Painting'
JISOA, II (1934) 106–14

TAGORE, A. N.   **46**
    'Likeness' (Sādriṣya)
JISOA, Golden Jubilee Number (1961) 1-11

TAGORE, A. N.   **47**
    'Ṣaḍāṅga : Six Limbs of Painting'
    (and other Essays on Indian Painting)
JISOA, Golden Jubilee Number (1961) 12-28; 96-97; 49-53; 1-11; 94-95;
40-48; 29-39 also published in book form under the title : 'SADĀNGA'
(Paris 1922).

TRIPATHI, D. D.   **48**
    '(The) Thirtytwo Sciences and the Sixtyfour Arts'
JISOA, XI (1943) 40-64.

2

GENERAL STUDIES
IN INDIAN PAINTING

BOOKS

AGRAWALA, V. S.   49
> 'Indian Miniatures : An Album'
(*New Delhi 1961*)

AGRAWAL, O. P.   50
> '(An) Introduction to Preservation of Paintings'
(*Baroda 1967*)

ANAND, MULK RAJ   51
> 'Album of Indian Painting'
(*NBT, New Delhi 1973*) *vi + 163, numerous mono and colour pls*
Covers a wide vista of Indian Painting, giving a bird's eye view of each style;
excellent visuals.

ARCHER, W. G.   52
> 'Indian Miniatures'
(*Greenwich 1967*) *with 100 pls (50 colour)*
Deals with medieval schools of Painting.

ARCHER, W. G.   53
> 'Indian Miniatures from the Mildred and W. G. Archer Collec-
> tion, Exhibition Catalogue'
(*Smithsonian Institution, Washington D. C. 1963*)

14

ARCHER, W. G.   54
'Indian Painting'
(*Batsford, London 1956*)

ARCHER, W. G.   55
'(The) Love of Krishna in Indian Painting and Poetry'
(*London 1957*)

ARNOLD. E. (tr.)   56
'Indian Miniature'
(*Paris 1968*)

ARNOLD, T. W. and WILKINSON, J. V. S.   57
'(The) Library of A. Chester Beatty, A Catalogue of the Indian Miniatures'
(*Oxford, London 1936*) *3 vols*

ASHTON, LEIGH (ed)   58
'(The) Art of India & Pakistan'
(*Faber & Faber London 1950*) *pp. 286, 8 colour pls 150 monotone*
A Com. catalogue of the exhibition at the Royal Academy of Art London 1947-48, articles by K de B. Codrington, John Irwin, Basil Gray and others; reviewed by H. Goetz in the **Marg**, V-2, 40-44.

BANERJEE, P.   59
'(The) Life of Krishna in Indian Art'
(*National Museum, New Delhi 1978*)
Study is largely based on miniature paintings.

BARRETT, D E. & GRAY, B.   60
'Painting of India'
(*Treasures of Asia Series, Skira, Cleveland 1963, reprinted Macmillan, London 1978*)
Very ably reviewed by Khandalavala in the **LK.** 11 (April 1962) 62-66; it should be taken as part of the monograph.

BHATTACHARYA, A. K.   61
'Technique of Indian Painting'
(*Calcutta 1976*) *pp. 174, 28 pls*

BINNEY, E.   62
'Persian and Indian Miniatures from the Collection of Edwin Binney 3rd'
(*Exhibited at the Portland Art Museum, 1962*)

BINYON, LAURENCE   63
'Asiatic Art : Sculpture & Painting'
Reprinted New Delhi 1981 pp. 71, 66 pls (London 1925) See review IJ

BROWN, PERCY   64
'Indian Painting'
(*New Delhi 1965*)
A useful survey of Indian Painting from the earliest times to the modern age.

BUSSAGALI, MARIO   65
'Indian Miniatures'
(*London 1966*)

CHAITANYA, KRISHNA   66
'(A) History of Indian Painting: Manuscript, Mughal and
Deccani Traditions'
(*Abhinav, New Delhi 1979) pp. xi + 91, 90 pls (10 Colour*)

CODRINGTON, K. de B.   67
'Study of Indian Art'
(*London 1944*)

COOMARASWAMY A. K.   68
'Catalogue of the Indian Collections in the Museum of Fine
Arts Boston'
6 Parts
(*Cambridge, Mass. 1926–30*)

COOMARASWAMY, A. K.   69
'Indian Drawings'
2 vols
(*London 1910–1912, reprinted BPH Varanasi 1979) Vol. I pp. 32 & 29
pls; Vol. II pp. 34 & 26 pls chiefly Rajput*)

COOMARASWAMY, A. K.   70
'Introduction to Indian Art'
(*Delhi 1969) with pls*
Deals with the growth and development of Indian art; chapters on 'Medieval
Buddhist Painting' (68-70); 'Jaina Painting' (71-72); 'Rajput Painting' (73-77)
and other related subjects.

COOMARASWAMY, A. K.   71
'Portfolio of Indian Art'
(*Museum of Fine Arts Boston Publication, Boston*)

COOMARASWAMY, A. K.   72
    'Yakṣas'
    2 vols in one
(*New Delhi 1971*)

CRESWELL, K. A. C.   73
    'A Bibliography of Painting in Islam'
(*Cairo 1953*)

CRESWELL, K. A. C.   74
    'A Bibliography of the Architecture, Arts and Crafts of Islam,
      to 1st January 1960'
(*The American University at Cairo Press, 1961*)
A grand work; includes a large number of entries in English, French and German; French and German works are not easily accessible in India; there are no entries from Hindi and other vernacular journals of India; much has since been published and it has to be adequately supplemented; in any case it remains the basic work, inevitable for any scholarly study of the subject.

DAS, A. K.   75
    'Treasures of Indian Painting'
(*Jaipur 1976*)

DWIVEDI, V. P.   76
    'Barahmasa'
(*New Delhi 1980*)
Depiction of Indian seasons in miniature Painting.

DUTT, M. N.   77
    'Dissertation of Painting'
(*Calcutta 1922*)

GANGOLY, O C.   78
    'Critical Catalogue of Miniature Paintings in the Baroda
      Museum'
(*Baroda 1961*)
Jaina, Pahari, Mughal, Deccani, Rajput and other schools and Rāga—Rāginī paintings.

GANGOLY, O. C.   79
    'Studies on Indian Art'
(*Ahmedabad 1953*) *pp. 118, 12 pls*

GANGULY, A. B.   80
'Fine Art in Ancient India'
(*New Delhi 1979*) *pp. 180, 23 pls*

GOETZ, H.   81
'Art of the World : India'
(*Bombay 1964*) *pp. 283 with pls & figs.*

GOETZ, H.   82
'Indian and Persian Miniature Paintings in the Rijksmuseum
    Amsterdam'
(*1958*)

GRAY, BASIL   83
'(The) Art of India and Pakistan'
(*London 1950*)

GRAY, B.   84
'Indian Miniatures'
(*Oxford, London 1959*)

GUPTA, S. N.   85
'Catalogue of Indian Paintings in the Central Museum Lahore'
(*Calcutta 1922*)

HAVELL, E. B.   86
'(The) Art Heritage of India'
(*Taraporevala, Bombay 1964) comprising of his two works : 'Indian Sculp-
ture & Painting' and 'Ideals of Indian Art' : revised by Pramod Chandra.*
A separate section on Indian Painting, Part—I, Chapters X—XIII, pp. 65-109 and
a very useful Appendix : 'The Indian Process of Fresco Buono—An Outline of
Rajasthani Painting' by Dr. Pramod Chandra, pp. 110-118.

HAZEK, L.   87
'Miniatures from the East'
(*London 1960*)

KALA, S. C.   88
'Indian Miniatures in the Allahabad Museum'
(*Allahabad 1961*) *pp. 12, 3 colour and 22 mono pls*
Reviewed in the **LK** No. 10 (Oct. 1961) p. 61.

KENNEDY, J. F.   89
    'Indian Painting'
(*London 1965*)

KHANDALAVALA, KARL J.   90
    'Development of Style in Indian Painting'
(*Bombay 1974*) *pp. 99, 16 pls*
Deals with paintings of the earliest times to Ajanta, the Aftermath of Ajanta and the Mughal School; a very scholarly work; reviewed in the **LK** No.18 p.45.

KHANDALAVALA, KARL J.   91
    'Indian Sculpture & Painting'
(*Bombay 1938*)

KHANDALAVALA, KARL J. & MOTICHANDRA   92
    'Miniatures and Sculptures from the Collection of the Late Sir
      Cowasji Jehangir'
(*Bombay 1965*)

**KHANDALAVALA, KARL J., MOTICHANDRA &
PRAMODCHANDRA**   93
    'Miniature Paintings from the Sri Motichand Khajanchi
      Collection'
(*Lalit Kala Akademi, New Delhi 1960*)
Reviewed in the **LK** No. 9 (April 1961) 65-66.

KRAMRISCH, STELLA   94
    (The) Art of India' (Through the Ages)
(*London 1965*) *pp. 240, 190 pls*
Traditions of Indian Sculpture, Painting and Architecture.

KRAMRISCH, STELLA   95
    'Indian Art & Art-Crafts'
(*Madras 1923*)

LILLYS, WILLIAM & OTHERS   96
    'Oriental Miniatures'
(*London 1965*) *pp 102*

MEHTA, N. C.   96—A
    'Bharatiya Chitra-kala' (Hindi)
(*Allahabad 1933*)

MEHTA, N. C.   97
    'Studies in Indian Painting'
(*Bombay 1926*)

MOOKERJI, AJIT   98
    'Art of India'
(*Calcutta 1966*) *pp. 152*

MOOKERJI, AJIT   99
    'Tantra Art : Its Philosophy & Physics'
(*New Delhi 1966*)
Also includes a study of the concerned paintings which abound in all indigenous styles.

MOTICHANDRA   100
    'Indian Art'
(*Prince of Wales Museum of W. I. Bombay 1964*) *xx+43. 34 pls*
An excellent treatment of Western Indian, Sultanate, Mughal, Rajasthani and Deccani Paintings with reference to the miniatures preserved in the Prince of Wales Museum of W. I. Bombay.

PAL, PRATAPADITYA   101
    'Indo-Asian Art from the John Gilmore Ford Collection'
(*Baltimore, Maryland 1971*)
A Catalogue of the Exhibition at the Walters Art Gallery Baltimore; Reviewed in the **LK** No. 17, p. 47.

PAL, P. & GLYNN, C.   102
    ·(The) Sensuous Line : Indian Drawings from the Paul F. Walter Collection
(*Los Angeles County Museum of Art, Los Angeles 1976*)

PRASAD, USHA   103
    'Indian Painting : A Romance'
(*New Delhi*)

RAI KRISHNADAS   104
    'Bharat-ki-Chitrakala' (Hindi)
(*Allahabad 1974*
A very learned yet simple history of Indian Painting through the Ages.

RANDHAWA, M. S. & GALBRAITH, J. K.   105
    'Indian Painting, the Scene Themes and Legends'
(*Boston 1968*)

RAWSON, PHILIP S.   106
    'Indian Painting'
(*London 1961*)

ROWLAND, BENJAMIN   107
    '(The) Art & Architecture of India'
(*London 1953*)
Along with Architecture it also deals with Painting

SHARMA, O. P.   108
    'Indian Miniature Painting'
(*Tokyo 1973*)

SIVARAMAMURTI, C.   109
    'Indian Painting'
(*NBT, New Delhi 1970*)
Mainly deals with Ancient Indian Painting, particularly with South Indian styles,
a brief but very learned enumeration.

SIVARAMAMURTI, C.   110
    'Nataraja in Art, Thought and Literature'
(*Delhi 1974*)

SIVARAMAMURTI, C.   111
    '(The) Painter in Ancient India'
(*Abhinav, New Delhi 1978*) *Pp. 93, 70 Pls*

SIVARAMAMURTI, C.   112
    'Sanskrit Literature and Art : Mirrors of Indian Culture'
(*Delhi 1955*)
Valuable literary references which are relevant to the study of Indian Painting.

SIVARAMAMURTI, C.   113
    'Some Aspects of Indian Culture'
(*Delhi 1969*)

SIVARAMAMURTI, C.   114
    'South Indian Paintings'
(*National Museum, New Delhi 1968*)
Reviewed by Khandalavala in the **LK** No.15 (1972) 64-65.

SKELTON, R.   115
    'Indian Miniatures from the 15th–19th Centuries'
(*Venice 1961*)

SMITH, VINCENT A.   **116**
    '(A) History of Fine Art in India and Ceylon'
(3rd ed. revised by Karl J. Khandalavala, Taraporevala Bombay 1969)
with pls
Chapter—VIII 'Early Schools of Indian Painting' (Ajanta & Bagh, pp.85-101) and
Chapter—XV 'Painting' (The Gujarati School and Mughal Painting pp. 180-208)
are very useful.

TAKATA, OSAMU & VENO, TIRUO   **117**
    '(The) Art of India'
(Tokyo 1966)

TAKI, S.   **118**
    'An Example of the Earliest Indian Painting'
(Tokyo, 1919)

TAKI, S.   **119**
    'Three Essays in Oriental Painting'
(London 1910)

THOMAS, P.   **120**
    'Incredible India'
(Taraporevala, Bombay 1966)
Mystic practices and their depiction in Art.

TIWARI, R. P.   **121**
    'Survey of Drawing in Ancient India'
(Delhi 1973)

VATSYAYAN, KAPILA   **122**
    '(The) Dance in Indian Painting'
(Abhinav, New Delhi)

WELCH, S. C.   **123**
    'A Flower from Every Meadow : Indian Paintings from
       American Collections'
(New York 1973)

WELCH, S. C.   **124**
    'Indian Drawings and Painted Sketches'
    (16th through 19th centuries)
(New York 1976)
Of Mughal, Rajput, Deccanese and other schools; an excellent work with superb
visuals.

WILKINSON, J. V. S.   **125**
>'(The) Library of A. Chester Beatty. A Catalogue of the Indian
>Miniatures'
>3 vols

(*London 1936*)

WINSTEDT, RICHARD (ed.)   **126**
>'Indian Art'

(*Faber & Faber, London 1947*)
Article on Indian Painting by J. V. S. Wilkinson, pp. 103-50, mainly deals with Mughal and post Mughal styles.

ZIMMER, HEINRICH   **127**
>'Art of Indian Asia'
>Vol. I. (Text) Vol. II (Plates)

(*tr. C. J. Campbell, New York 1964*) *pp. 490, 614 pls*
A very learned enumeration of Indian Art.

—   **127 A**

>'Islamic Heritage of India'

(*National Museum New Delhi 1981*) *Pp. 64, 21 pls*
Catalogue listing 126 Arabic & Persian Mss., 71 Miniature paintings, coins, textiles and carpets, and arms; a very learned Introduction by Karl J. Khandalavala pp. 1-12.

—   **128**

>'Manuscripts from Indian Collections : Descriptive Catalogue'

(*National Museum, New Delhi 1964*) *with pls*
Including illustrated mss. containing miniatures of different schools 14th to 18th century.

—   **129**

>'Museums & Art Galleries'

(*Publication Division New Delhi 1956*) *with pls*
A section on 'Indian Paintings'; useful references to miniatures preserved in various parts of the country.

—   **130**

>'Museum & Picture Gallery Baroda : Guide to the'

(*Baroda, n. d.*) *with pls*
Includes references to miniature paintings and painted textiles.

—   131

'Panorama of Indian Painting'
(*Publication Division, New Delhi 1968*)
Learned articles by O.C. Gangoly, Motichandra, Niharranjan Ray,M.S. Randhawa
and others.

—   132

'Persian & Indian Miniatures'
(*Portland 1962*)
Catalogue of Exhibition at Portland Art Museum   with 4 colour and 19 mono pls;
reviewed by Khandalavala in the **LK** No. 11 (April 1962) 69-70.

ARTICLES

AGARWAL, O. P.   133
'(A) Study of the Technique and Materials of Indian Illustrated
Mss.'
NMB, No. 3 (1972) 22-33
An important paper dealing with writing material, pigments and other technical
aspects, with excellent pls.

ANAND, M. R.   134
'What is Painting'
MARG, XXV-4 (Sept 1972) 53-76, 19 excellent pls
Survey from Ajanta to contemporary art.

CHATTOPADHYAYA, CHAITANYADEV   135
'Art from the Point of view of the Artist'
JISOA, XI (1943) 32-39

COOMARASWAMY, A. K.   136
'Nāgara Painting'
RUPAM, No. 37 (Jan 1929) 24-28
A very learned and useful article by one of the greatest scholars of the subject.

COOMARASWAMY, A. K.   137
'Renaissance of Indian Culture'
JISOA, XV (1947) 7-9

COOMARASWAMY, A. K. 138
 '(The) Technique and Theory of Indian Painting'
Technical Studies in the Field of the Fine Arts
Harvard, III (1934)

COOMARASWAMY, A. K. 139
 '(The) Traditional Conception of Ideal Portraiture'
JISOA, VII (1939) 74–82

GANGOLY, O. C. 140
 'Presidential Address : Sculpture & Painting Section (Fine
  Arts) 10th Session AIOC 1939 Tirupati'
AIOC, X (1939) 538–52
On some basic problems of Indian Art.

GHOSE, AJIT 141
 '(A) Comparative Survey of Indian Painting'
IHQ, II–2 (1926) 299–312

GHOSH, J. C. 142
 'Classification of Painting'
ABORI, XIX (1937–38) 81–82

GHOSH, M. R. 143
 'Archaeological Evidence in Support of the Origin and Develop-
  ment of Indian Painting and Musical Instruments from Ancient
  Times'
AIOC, VI (1930) 241–42

GOETZ, H. 144
 'Indian Miniature Paintings'
BMB, VII (1949–50) 53–66

GOETZ, H. 145
 'Indian Paintings in German Collections'
Eastern Art, II (1930) 142–66

GOETZ, H. 146
 'Indian Painting in the Muslim Period : A Revised Historical
  Outline'
JISOA, XV (1947) 19–41 and pls
An extremely useful survey.

GOETZ, H.   **147**
> 'Presidential Address, Technical Sciences & Fine Arts Section
> XVII Session AIOC Ahmedabad : The Application of Modern
> Research Methods to the Study of Indian Art'

AIOC, XVII (1953) 191-94

GOETZ, H.   **148**
> '(The) Relations between Indian Painting and Culture'

RUPAM, 22-23 (1925) 46-54

JAIN, RAMESH   **149**
> 'Abhiprayon-ka-Lokikaran' (Hindi)

RB, XIII-4 (Sept 1971) 63-70
Motifs of Indian Art vis-a-vis the basic human sentiments; an interesting study.

JINAVIJAYA, MUNI   **150**
> 'Chitra-Parichaya' (Hindi)

Bharatiya Vidya, III-1, 235-40
Introduction to Indian Painting.

JOHNSON, B. B.   **151**
> '(A) Preliminary Study of the Technique of Indian Miniature
> Painting'

in **'Aspects of Indian Art'** *(ed. P. Pal, Brill Leiden 1972) 139-46, 15 pls*

KHANDALAVALA, KARL J.   **152**
> '(The) Development of Style in Indian Painting'
> (From the earliest Times till Ajanta)

IB, IX-2 (Sept 1972) 89-100, 2 pls
A very learned enumeration of early Indian Painting.

KRAMRISCH, STELLA   **153**
> 'Presidential Address : Fine Arts Section AIOC, 9th Session
> 1937, Trivandrum'

AIOC, IX (1937) 1029-40
On the Theory of Indian Art.

MAITRA, A. K.   **154**
> 'Aims and Methods of Painting in Ancient India'

RUPAM, 13-14 (Jan-June 1923) 19-27

MANUK, P. C.   **155**
'(An) Address on Indian Painting'
JBORS, IX (1923) 23-29

MEHTA, N. C.   **156**
'Notes on Indian Painting'
*AIOC, V-2 (Lahore 1928) 1059-70; also published in the JIH, VII-1
(April 1928) 9-12*

MITTAL, JAGDISH   **157**
'Islamic Painting of the North and the Deccan'
Roop-Lekha, *XXXVIII (M.S. Randhawa Presentation Vol.) 128-38, 11 pls*
A useful survey of Indian Painting including Jaina, Sultanate, Mughal and
Deccanese.

MOOKERJEE, MONOTOSH   **158**
'Two Illuminated Mss. in the Asutosh Museum of Indian Art'
JISOA, XV (1947) 89-99

NATH, R.   **159**
'Lahara-Vallari in Indian Art'
IMB, X-2 (July 1975) 57-70, 12 pls
A popular motif depicted in Indian Painting (e. g. Ajanta) and Carvings.

PARIMAL, PRAKASH   **160**
'Bharatiya kala men Samskritik Abhipraya evam Chitrarudi ke
Lokikaran ki Prakriya'
(Hindi)
RB, combined Vols. XII-XIII (1970) 161-83
Deals ably with motifs, designs and subjects of Indian Art particularly Indian
Painting, from aesthetic point of view, with Sastric background.

SAHAI, Y.   **161**
'(The) Costumes of Dancers in Indian Paintings'
RJ, XII-XIII (1972-73) 39-46

SAHAL, KANHIYALAL   **162**
'Abhipraya aur Kathanak Rudhi-ek
Punar mulyankana' (Hindi)
RB, Combined vols XII-XIII (1970) 195-200
Motifs and their aesthetic criticism; a very interesting article.

SHASTRI, HIRANAND 163
'Indian Pictorial Art as revealed in
Book Illustrations'
AIOC, V-2 (1928) 1108-10

SHASTRI, HIRANAND 164
'Some Waslis'
JISOA, VIII (1940) 56-61

SHERWANI, H. K. 165
'Medieval Indian Painting'
IB, III-2 (Sept 1966) 113-24
A very good appraisal.

SIVARAMAMURTI, C. 166
'Artists' Materials'
Calcutta Oriental Journal, II (1935)

SIVARAMAMURTI, C. 167
'(The) Indian Painter and his Art'
Cultural Heritage of India, *Vol. III Ramakrishna Mission Calcutta
(1936)*

TAGORE, RABINDRA NATH 168
'(The) Creative Ideal'
RUPAM, 9 (Jan 1922) 5-7

VREDENBERG, E. 169
'(The) Continuity of Pictorial Tradition in the
Art of India'
RUPAM, No. 1 (1920)

WARD, W. E. 170
'Three Indian Paintings'
Bulletin of the Cleveland Museum of Art, Jan. 1953

WILKINSON, J. V. S. & GRAY, B. 171
'Indian Paintings in a Persian Museum,
The Burlington Magazine, *Vol. 66 (1935)*

WOODROFFE, SIR JOHN (ARTHUR AVALON)   **172**
'(The) Indian Magna Mater'
IAL, II. 1-2 (1926) 66-89

A wonderful monograph on the artistic depiction of some concepts of Śāktism, e. g. the symbolism of the Bindu. Pl. III depicts Devi on a heap of corpses with amputed limbs similar to some mural paintings of Fatehpur Sikri. The former may provide a key to understand the latter. The article also holds key to understand some mystic Pahari miniature paintings.

3

MURAL PAINTING
(A) Ancient

BOOKS

BUSSAGALI, MARIO 178
'Painting of Central Asia'
(*tr. from Italian by L. Small, Treasures of the Asia Series,
Geneva 1963*)

CHAITANYA, KRISHNA 179
'(A) History of Indian Painting : The Mural Tradition'
(*Abhinav, New Delhi 1976*), *70 pls*

CHAKRABARTI, J. 180
'Techniques in Indian Mural Painting'
(*Calcutta 1980*) *pp. 150, 25 pls*

CHITRA, V. R. & SRINIVASAN, T. N. 181
'Cochin Murals'
2 vols
(*Bombay 1940*)

DEY, MUKUL CHANDRA 182
'My Pilgrimage to Ajanta and Bagh'
(*London 1925*)

DHAVALIKAR, M. K. 183
'Ajanta : A Cultural Study'
(*University of Poona, Poona 1974*)
Based on the study of the Paintings of Ajanta.

DIKSHIT, S. K. 184
'Central Archaeological Museum Gwalior : A Guide to–'
(*Gwalior 1962*) *with pls*
Copies of Bagh paintings; also deals with the paintings of the Mughal period.

FERGUSSON, J & BURGESS, J. 185
'(The) Cave Temples of India'
(*London 1880*)
Mainly on Ajanta.

GHOSH, A. 186
'Ajanta Murals'
(*A. S. I. New Delhi 1967*) *with colour pls*
A very useful survey; reviewed by Khandalavala in the **LK**, No. 14 (1969) 61-62.

GILL, R.   187
'Buddhist Caves of Ajanta'
(Revised by J. Burgess, London 1876)

GOETZ, H.   188
'Ajanta Portfolio'
(NBT, New Delhi 1964) pp. 5 with 6 colour pls.

GRIFFITHS, JOHN   189
'Paintings in the Buddhist Cave Temples of Ajanta'
2 vols : Vol. I Pictorial Subjects
II Decorative Details
(London 1896-97)

GUPTE, R. S & MAHAJAN, B. D.   190
'Ajanta Ellora & Aurangabad Caves'
(Taraporevala Bombay 1962) numerous pls
Deals with Architecture and Paintings of these ancient sites.

HACKIN, J.   191
'Buddhist Art in Central Asia'
(London 1937)

HERRINGHAM, LADY C.   192
'Ajanta Frescoes'
2 vols
(India Society, London 1915)

JOUVEAU-DUBREUIL, G.   193
'Fresco-Painting at Sittannavasal'
(Pudukkottai 1920)
7th century mural painting; also see S. R. Balasubrahmanyam **JOR.** IX—1 (1935)
on this subject.

KHARE, MAHESHWARI DAYAL   194
'Bagh-ki-Guphayen' (Hindi)
(Madhya Pradesh Hindi Academy, Bhopal 1971) 62 pls and a few very useful plans of the Bagh caves

MADANJEET SINGH   195
'Himalayan Art'
(*Macmillan, London 1968*)
Wall Paintings of Ladakh, Lahaul, Spiti, Nepal, Sikkim and Bhutan, 11th to 18th century A. D. a very helpful survey.

MADANJEET SINGH   196
'India : Paintings from Ajanta Caves'
(*Unesco, Paris 1954*)

MARSHALL, JOHN   197
'Bagh Caves'
(*London 1927*) *numerous pls*
Basic work on the paintings of the Bagh caves of the Gupta period.

RICE, T. T.   198
'Ancient Arts of Central Asia'
(*London 1965*)
Valuable references to Buddhist paintings.

ROWLAND, BENJAMIN   199
'(The) Ajanta Caves'
(Early Buddhist Paintings from India)
(*Unesco, 1963*)
A brief but useful survey.

ROWLAND, BENJAMIN & COOMARASWAMY, A. K.   200
'(The) Wall Paintings of India, Central Asia & Ceylon : A
Comparative Study'
(*Boston 1938*)

SIVARAMAMURTI, C.   201
'South Indian Paintings'
(*National Museum, New Delhi 1968*) *107 pls*
Though it also deals with miniature paintings, mostly it covers murals.

STEIN, AUREL   202
(1) 'Ancient Khotan' (*Oxford 1907*)
(2) 'Serindia' (*Oxford 1921*)
(3) 'On Central Asian Tracks' (*London 1933*)
Valuable references to Buddhist paintings (Mural).

YAZDANI, G.   **203**
> 'History of the Deccan'
> Vol. I   Part–VIII Fine Arts

(London 1953) *with pls*
Its Chapter—IV deals with wall paintings of Ajanta.

YAZDANI, G.   **204**
> 'Ajanta'
> 4 vols

(London 1930–55)

—   **205**

> 'Ajanta Paintings'

(Lalit Kala Akademi, New Delhi 1956) *20 colour pls*
Excellent visuals; one-page Introduction by Ashfaque Hussain is also interesting.

—   **206**

> 'Annual Reports of the Archaeological Survey of India,
> 1902-3 to 1936–37

References to wall paintings in various parts of the country, under conservation; in some cases this is the basic data of research.

—   **207**

> 'Indian Archaeology : A Review'
> 1953–54 to 1977–78

Each volume has one or two sections on the preservation of mouments containing very valuable references to Mural Paintings of India from 1st century B. C. to 19th century A. D.. e. g. 1954-55, pp. 48-50, references to Mural paintings of Bagh, Badami, Ajanta, Ellora, Aurangabad, Tirumalai, Sittanavasal, Tanjore, Cochin, Bijapur, Chanda etc (with pls); 1955-56, pp. 54-55, references to Mural paintings of Ajanta, Baroda, Agra, Cochin etc. (with pls); 1956-57, pp. 65-66, references to Mural paintings of Bagh, Ajanta, Ellora, Agra, Baroda, Chanda and other sites (with pls); 1957-58, pp. 108-110, Ajanta, Ellora, Chanda, Agra. Allahabad etc (with pls) and so on.

—   **208**

> 'Reports of the A. S. I.'

(Cunningham Series) 23 vols, 1862–84 and Index to these vols. by V. A. Smith (Calcutta 1887)
Survey of Ancient and Medieval monuments of India including sites of wall-paintings (both ancient and medieval). The series has been reprinted (IBH, Varanasi 1972). These volumes provide the basic data for research in art, architecture archaeology and other disciplines of Indological studies.

ARTICLES

CHAMPAKALAKSHMI, R.   217
    'New Light on the Chola Frescoes of Tanjore'
JIH, Golden Jubilee Vol. (1973) 349-59, 21 pls and 1 plan

COOMARASWAMY, A. K.   218
    '(The) Painter's Art in Ancient India : Ajanta'
JISOA, I (1933) 26-29

COUSINS, J. H.   219
    'Post Ajanta Mural Paintings'
AIOC, IX (Trivandrum 1937) 44-46

DHAVALIKAR, M. K.   220
    'Sri-Yugadhara-A Master Artist of Ajanta'
AA, XXXI. 4 (1969) 301-8, 1 pl
On the basis of a short epigraph which reads : **'Śrī-Yugadhara Śūtradhāra'**; the author's analysis of the term is also useful.

DUPREE, N. H.   221
    '(The) Colossal Buddhas and the Monastic Grottos'
MARG, XXIV-2 (March 1971) 17-24 and pls
Valuable references to Buddhist Mural paintings in the rock-cut caves of Bamiyan (Afghanistan).

FABRI, CHARLES   222
    'Frescoes of Ajanta'
MARG, IX-1 (Dec 1955) 61-76 and 8 pls, 9 line-sketches of painting
A very learned article.

GANGOLY, O. C.   223
    'Discoveries of Chola Frescoes in Tanjore'
IAL, IX. 1-2 (1935) 86-91

GANGOLY, O. C.   224
    'Summary Survey of Orissan Painting'
MARG, VIII-4 (Sept 1955) 47-56. 6 pls and 7 figs
On the frescoes and books-illustrations, from 2nd century B. C. to 19th century A. D.

GODE, P. K.   225
    'Rangavalli kala ka Itihas' (Hindi)
    (50 A. D. to 1900 A. D)
NPP, LIII-1 (V. S. 2005) 1-17)
On Rangolī or Alpanā; he also discusses various types of mural paintings; a very learned article; also see Baldeva Upadhyaya's Note on this subject in **NPP LIII-2** (V. S. 2005) p. 129.

GOETZ, H.   226
'(The) Golden Age of Buddhist Art : Painting (Ajanta)'
MARG, IX-2 (March 1956) 86-92, 10 pls (8 colour)
An excellent article.

GOVINDASWAMI, S. K.   227
'Cola Painting'
JISOA, I (1933) 73-80

GUPTA, S. P.   228
'Foreign Influence in the Buddhist Paintings from Khotan
   Central Asia'
RJ, VII-IX (1966-68) 41-46

·HUNTINGTON, J. C.   229
'Gu-Ge Bris : A Stylistic Amalgam'
in **'Aspects of Indian Art'** *(ed. P. Pal, Brill, Leiden, 1972) 105-117,
12 pls*
Painting style, mainly mural, extending from Lahul-Spiti to Ladakh, from 11th
to 17th century.

JAIN, S. C.   230
'Sittannavasala' (Hindi)
JSB, V-2 (Sept 1938) 101-5
On the Jaina paintings of its caves.

JOUVEAU-DUBREUIL, G.   231
'Pallava Paintings'
Indian Antiquary, LII (1923) 45-47

KRAMRISCH, STELLA   232
'A Painted Ceiling'
JISOA, VII (1939) 175-84

KRAMRISCH, STELLA   233
'Paintings at Badami'
JISOA, IV (1936) 57-61 and VI (1938) 202-3

KRAMRISCH, STELLA   234
'Some Wall Paintings from Kelaniya'
IHQ, I-1 (1925) 111-16

LAL, B. B. 235
'Preservation of Mural Paintings'
AI, No. 22 (1966) 83-101, 21 pls
References to mural paintings of India from Ancient to Medieval times.

LEVINE, DEBORAH BROWN 236
'Aurangabad : A Stylistic Analysis'
AA, XXVIII. 2-3 (1966) 175-204, 21 pls and 5 figs of ground plans
Along with structural elements and sculptures he also deals with paintings of
these caves, contemporaneous to those of Ajanta.

MANUK, P. C. 237
'Ajanta'
JBORS, XI (1925) 109-27

MIRASHI, V. V. 238
'(The) Age of Bagh Caves'
IHQ, XXI-2 (1945) 79-85

MITRA, R. L. 239
'On Representation of Foreigners in the Ajanta Frescoes'
JASB, 1st Series, XLVII-1 (1878) 62-72, 4 pls

MONTGOMERY, E. & BASKARAN, S. T. 240
'(The) Armamalai Paintings'
LK, No. 16 (1974) 22-27, 7 pls and 2 figs
Cave Paintings of c. 9th century A. D.

PARAMSIVAN, S. 241
'(An) Investigation into the Methods of the Mural Paintings'
*JISOA, VII (1939) 18-27 (in Cochin and Travancore); 27-33 (Lepakshi
and Somapalayam); 33-38 (Tirumalai)*

PARAMSIVAN, S. 242
'Indian Wall Paintings'
Journal of the Madras University, XII (1940) and XIII (1941)

PARAMASIVAN, S. 243
'(The) Mural Paintings in the Brihadisvara Temple at
Tanjore—An Investigation into the Method'
Technical Studies, V (1937) 221-40

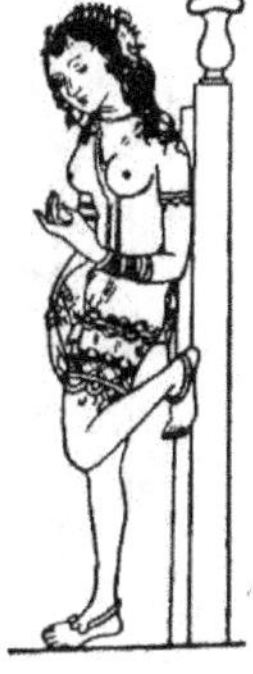

PARAMASIVAN, S.   **244**

'(A) Note on the Dating of the Frescoes in the Brahadisvara
Temple at Tanjore'
JOR, IX-4 (Oct–Dec 1935) 363–68
Çola and Nāyak paintings of c.12th and 17th century respectively; also see
K. A. Nilakantha Sastri's Note on Tanjore frescoes in the **JOR** X-1 (Jan-March
1936) p. 89.

PARAMASIVAN, S.   **245**

'(The) Pallava Paintings at Conjeevaram-An Investigation into
the Method'
Proceedings of Indian Academy of Sciences, X (1939)
Section-A, 77-84

PARAMASIVAN, S.   **246**

'Technique of the Painting Process in the Rock-cut Temples
of Badami'
Proceedings of Indian Academy of Sciences, X (1939)
Section-A, 145-49

PARAMASIVAN, S.   **247**

'Techniques of the Paintings Process in the Cave Temples of
Ajanta'
*Annual Report of the Archaeological Department of His Exalted Highness
the Nizam's Dominions, 1936-37 (1939) 25-30*

PARAMASIVAN, S.   **248**

'(The) Wall Paintings in the Bagh Caves—An Investigation
into their Methods'
Proceedings of Indian Academy of Sciences, X (1939) Section-A, 85-95

PARAMASIVAN, S.   **249**

'(The) Mural Paintings in the Cave Temple at Sittannavasal-
An Investigation into the Method'
Technical Studies, VIII-2 (1939) 82-89

PARANAVITANA, S.   **250**

'(The) Significance of the Paintings of Sigiri'
AA, XXIV. 3-4 (1961) 382-87
Earliest specimens of mural art in Ceylon.

PODUVAL, R. V.   251
　　'Note on Paintings and Sculptures in Travancore'
JISOA, V (1937) 181–83

RAMACHANDRAN, K. V.   252
　　'Paintings from Tiruvanjikulam'
Triveni Madras, Vol. IV (1931)

RAMACHANDRAN, T. N.   253
　　'Cave Temple and Paintings of Sittannavasal'
LK. 9 (April 1961) 30–54, 28 pls (4 colour) 1 fig.
An Excellent monograph on 7th century Mural painting site; see also note by
P. R. Srinivasan on the Date of these paintings in the same issue of the **LK,**
pp, 57-58; he places them in the first half of the 9th century.

RAMACHANDRAN, T. N.   254
　　'Cave Temples near Tirumalaipuram and their Paintings'
JISOA, IV (1936) 65–71

RAMACHANDRAN, T. N.   255
　　'Find of Tempera Paintings in Sitabhinji District, Keonjhar,
　　　Orissa'
AA, XIV. 1–2 (1951) 5–25, 10 pls
These could have been executed between 4th and 8th century A. D.

RAMACHANDRAN, T. N.   256
　　'Frescoes of Keonjargarh'
　　(Painting of Sitabhinji)
MARG, VIII-4 (Sept 1955) 57–63 and 3 pls
In Orissa; the article places them around the Gupta period.

RAMACHANDRAN, T. N.   257
　　'(The) Royal Artist Mahendravarman'
JOR, VII (1933) 219–46
Of the Pallava period, e. g. Sittannavasal, c. 7th century A. D.

RAMAN, K. V.   258
　　'Vijaynagar Paintings at Kanchi'
IH, IV-1 (Jan–June 1976) 71–73, 3 pls
Small but interesting article dealing with mural painting of Varadarājāswāmin
Temple at Kanchipuram.

RAY, NIHAR RANJAN   259
'Paintings at Pagan'
JISOA, VI (1938) 137–48

ROWLAND, BENJAMIN   260
'(The) Wall–Paintings of Bamiyan'
MARG, XXIV-2 (March 1971) 25-50, 15 pls
Buddhist paintings in the rock-cut caves of Bamiyan.

SARMA, M. S. SUNDARA   261
'Sittannavasal Frescoes'
Triveni Madras, III–1 (1930)

SAUNDERS, KENNETH   262
'(The) Living Tradition of Ajanta'
RUPAM, No. 41 (Jan 1930) 11-14

SAXENA, B. D.   263
'Meri Bagh Yatra' (Hindi)
MPS, Vol. 66 No. 29 (Purātatva Aṅka) (June 1970) 66-67, 2 pls
Deals with Bagh Caves and its paintings

SCHLINGLOFF, DIETER   264
'Kalyanakarin's Adventures, the Identification of An Ajanta
        Paintings'
AA, XXXVIII. 1 (1976) 5–28, 2 pls and 29 figs
A very learned article on identification of a theme; also deals with Ancient Indian
sailing vessels.

SHARMA, V. V.   265
'Method of Plastering Walls for Painting'
(Sudhālepa Vidhānam)
IHQ, III–1 (1927) 53-59

SIVARAMAMURTI, C   266
'Mural Paintings'
in '**Jaina Art and Architecture**' *(Bharatiya Jnanpitha New Delhi 1974, ed.
by A. Ghosh) Vol II. 381-89, 2 figs, 7 monochrome and 21 colour pls*
Jaina paintings of South India as Ellora, Sittanavasal etc.

SIVARAMAMURI C.   267
'Note on the Paintings at Tirumalaipuram'
JISOA, IV (1936) 72-74

SIVARAMAMURTI, C, 268
'Paintings from Lepakshi'
JISOA, V (1937) 184-87

SIVARAMAMURTI, C. 269
'Some Frescoes of the Cholas'
Triveni Madras, Vol. VI (1932)

SIVARAMAMURTI, C. 270
'Western Chalukya Paintings at Badami'
LK, No. 5 (April 1959) 49-58, 12 pls (2 colour)
Mural painting of the period 578-579 A. D.

SPINK, WALTER M. 271
'Ajanta : A Brief History'
in **'Aspects of Indian Art'** *(ed. by P. Pal, Brill Leiden 1972) 49-58,*
10 pls

SPINK, WALTER M. 272
'Ajanta's Chronology : Politics and Patronage'
in **'Kalādarsana'** *(American Studies in the Art of India) (American Institute of Indian Studies New Delhi 1981) 109-26, 11 pls, 5 diagrams and figs.*

SRINIVASAN, P. R. 273
'Early Pallava Paintings at Panamalai and their Relationship
    to the Paintings at Sittannavasal'
AIOC, XVIII (Annamalai 1955) 328-40

THOMSON, D V. (Jr) 274
'Preliminary Notes on Some Early Hindu Paintings at Ellora'
RUPAM, No. 26 (April 1926) 45-48

TUCCI, GIUSEPPE 275
'Indian Paintings in Western Tibetan Temples'
AA, VII 1-4 (1937 191-205, 15 pls
Mural paintings at Man-Nana; typically Indian in style and contents c. 10th-11th century.

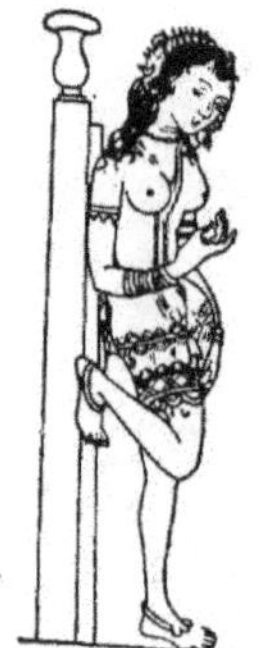

VENKATA RAMAN, K. R.   276
'A Note on the Sittannavasal and Kudumiyamalai Monuments'
JIH, XXXIII-3 (1955) 347–55
Tries to settle the chronology of these paintings.

WARD, WILLIAM E.   277
'Recently discovered Mahiyangana Paintings'
AA, XV 1-2 (1952) 108–13, 8 pls
Mural paintings in Ceylon of the period from 8th to 11th century A. D.

3

MURAL PAINTING
(B) Medieval
(MUGHAL, RAJPUT, PAHARI & DECCANI)

BOOKS

AGARWAL, RAM AVATAR   278
> 'History, Art & Architecture of Jaisalmer'

(New Delhi 1979) pp. 98 and pls
Along with architecture, it also deals with Mural and Miniature paintings of
Jaisalmer.

AGARWAL, RAM AVATAR   279
> 'Marwar Murals'

(New Delhi 1977)
Catalogues the mural paintings of the region, e. g. Jodhpur (Palaces, Havelis
Temples etc), Mandor, Nagaur, Didwana, Pali, Osia, Phalodi, Ghanerao etc.

ARYAN, K. C.   280
> 'Punjab Murals'

(New Delhi) pp. 130, xi+110 pls
On the wall-paintings of Punjab from late 18th to early 20th century A. D.

COLE, H. H.   281
> 'Preservation of National Monuments : Agra and Gwalior'

(Delhi 1885)
Mural paintings of the Tomb of Itmād'ud-Daulah Agra.

COLE, H. H.   282
> 'Preservation of National Monuments : Delhi'

(Delhi 1884)
Mural paintings of the Dīwān-i-Khāṣ Red Fort Delhi.

COUSENS, HENRY   283
‘Bijapur and its Architectural Remains’
(*A. S. I. Vol. 37, Imperial Series, Bombay 1916*) *numerous pls and figs.*
Along with architecture, it also deals with figurative mural paintings, e. g.
in the water-pavilions of Kumatgi, and the Ashar-Mahall.

GUPTE, TARAMATI   284
‘Mural Decorations in Kirtti–Mandir’ (Baroda)
in ‘**Gaekwad Cenotaphs**’ (*Baroda 1947*) *30–35, 5 pls*
Very much done in the living tradition of Ajanta in fresco and tempera by Nandlal
Bose; excellent specimens of Modern murals.

KHANDALAVALA, KARL J.   285
‘Wall Paintings from Amber’ (Portfolio)
(*Lalit Kala Akademi New Delhi 1974*) *6 pls & 1–4 pages*
Reviewed in the **LK** No. 18, p. 43; mural paintings from the so-called Bharmal’s
Chhatri at Amer (Jaipur); it is in fact the Chhatri of Raja Mansingh.

NATH, R.   286
‘Agra & Its Monumental Glory’
(*Taraporevala, Bombay 1977*)
References to Mural stylized paintings in the Mughal buildings of Agra.

NATH, R.   287
‘Colour Decoration in Mughal Architecture’
(*Taraporevala Bombay 1977*)
Chapter ‘Stucco and Architectural Painting’ pp. 42-65 (with pls) deals with
Mughal mural painting with a detailed historical background.

NATH, R.   288
‘History of Decorative Art in Mughal Architecture’
(*Moti–Banarsi Delhi 1977*)
Valuable references to various motifs and designs used in Mughal mural painting.

NATH, R.   289
‘(The) Immortal Taj Mahal’
(*Taraporevala Bombay 1972*)
Its pages 73-75 (3 pls) deal with incised Mural painting at the Taj Mahal; a
deshi technique as distinguished from Italian sgriffito.

SATYA PRAKASH   290
‘Bairat : A Bird’s Eye View’
(*Jaipur 1951*)
Fresco paintings of the Mughal period near Jaipur (Rajasthan).

SETH, MIRA   291
    'Wall Paintings of Western Himalayas'
With 32 colour and 86 mono pls

SMITH, E. W.   292
    'Akbar's Tomb at Sikandarah Agra'
A. S. I. New Imperial Series, Vol. XXXV (Allahabad 1909)
The tomb was built in 1605-12; the work deals with mural paintings also, in floral, stylized and arabesque designs.

SMITH, E. W.   293
    '(The) Moghul Architecture of Fatehpur Sikri'
A. S. I. New Imperial Series, Vol. XVIII, Parts I-IV (Allahabad 1894-98)
Part—I deals with frescoes of Khwabgah and Mariam's House; II with murals of the so-called Palace of Jodhbai; III with murals of Salim Chishti's Tomb, Hammams; and IV with the mural paintings of the Jami Masjid; the figurative art is in the residential palaces also; the work contains excellent drawings and colour reproductions, which it is hard to do in the 20th century.

SMITH, E. W.   294
    'Moghul Colour Decoration of Agra'
A. S. I. New Imperial Series Vol. XXX, Part-I (Allahabad 1901)
pp. 28, 103 pls
Deals with mural paintings of the Tomb of Itmad'ud-Daulah (1622-27) and the Chini-ka-Rauza (c.1639) at Agra. They consist of floral, arabesque and stylized designs-among the best of the Mughal murals; examples from the Chini-ka-Rauza, Itmad'ud-Daulah's Tomb and the Kanch-Mahal also reproduced in the **Journal of Indian Art London**, IX (1902) 71-79, 56 pls (53 colour); excellent drawing work.

ARTICLES

AGARWAL, O. P.   295
    'Technique of the Devi Mural at Kulu'
Studies in Museology, I (1965) 22-25

ANAND, M. R.   296
    'Some Notes on the Compositions of Pahari Murals'
MARG, XVII-3 (June 1964) 8-14
Much useful information.

ANAND, M. R.   297
    '(The) Techniques of the Fresco–Painting'
MARG, X-2 (March 1957) 27-29, 3 pls
In the Punjab.

ANAND, M. R.   298
    '(The) Tradition of Wall–Painting in Kerala'
MARG, XXXII-2 (March 1979) 37-54, 21 pls (11 colour)

ANAND, M. R.   299
    'Wall Paintings (of Himachal Pradesh)'
MARG, XXIII-2 (March 1970) 17-18 (and flaps) 2 pls

ARYAN, K. C. & GAIROLA, T. R.   300
    'Technical Notes'
    (On Pahari Wall Paintings)
MARG, XVII-3 (June 1964) 15–16

BAHURA, GOPAL NARAYAN   301
    'Amer Sthit Mansingh Mahal ke Bhitti–Chitra'
    (Katipaya Samsamayik Saksya) (Hindi)
RJ, XII–XIII (1972-73) 63-70
A very important paper on mural paintings of the Palace of Raja Mansingh at Amer, Jaipur; the learned author gives valuable contemporary literary evidence.

CHAKRAVARTI, P. L.   302
    'Chavanda-ki-Puratatvika Sampada' (Hindi)
SP, XXVIII–2 (April–June 1977) 43–47
Along with architecture, it also deals with Mural painting (in Mewar).

FRENCH, J. C.   303
    'Kangra Frescoes'
Indian Art & Letters, XXII (1948) 57-59

GAIROLA. T. R.   304
    'Wall Paintings from Rangmahal Chamba and Their
    Preservation'
Studies in Museology, IV (1968) 9-24

GOETZ, H.   305
    'Bundela Art'
JISOA, VI (1938) 181–94 & pls; reprinted RAA, 107-20 & pls
Mural paintings of Orchha and Datia etc.; a very learned and useful enumeration.

GOETZ, H. 306

'Decorative Mura s from Champaner'
Journal of the University of Bombay, XIX-2 (1950) 94-101, 5 pls
From the Ek-Mīnār-ki-Masjid Champaner.

GOETZ, H. 307

'(The) Early Rajput Murals of Bairat (A. D. 1587)'
ARS ORIENTALES, Washington Vol. I-1 (1954) 113-18 & 13 pls
reprinted RAA, 121-26 & pls
He studies them as Rajput with Mughal influence.

GOETZ H. 308

'(The) Nagaur School of Rajput Painting' (18th Century)
KALA NIDHI, 1 2 (1949); also published in AA, XII. 1-2 (1949)
89-98 & 4 pls
A very useful article on the set of Mural paintings in the Marwar region; allusions
to examples of other styles are enlightening and very interesting.

GOSWAMY, B. N. 309

'(The) Pindori Murals'
ROOP LEKHA, XLII. 1-2 (no date) 17-25, 10 pls
Seven miles east of Gurdaspur a religious place with Gaddi of the Mahant;
paintings of the Pahari school, first half of the 19th century; paurāṇic and
religious subjects.

GOSWAMY, KARUNA 310

'Frescoes in the Shish-Mahal at Patiala'
ROOP LEKHA, XXXVIII (M. S. Randhawa Presentation Vol)
120-27, 10 pls
Of mid-19th century depicting Śṛngāra, Bārahmāsā, Daśāvatāra and other
Purāṇic stories; of the Pahari School.

GUPTA, M. L. 310-A

'Nagaur Frescoes'
RJ Vol. I (n. d.) 33-36, no pls
Though small and descriptive, it is a useful article.

GUPTA, MOHANLAL 311

'Rajasthan-ke-Bhitti-Chitra' (Hindi)
PRHC, I (Jodhpur 1967) 234-36;
A brief appraisal of the Mural paintings of Rajasthan; the article also gives a list.

HOTCHAND 312
'Bhitti-Chitron-ka-Saranksana' (Hindi)
SP, XXV-1 (Jan–March 1974) 30–32
Preservation of mural paintings with reference to the paintings in Mansingh's Palace at Amer (Jaipur)

HOTCHAND 313
'Conservation of Wall Paintings at Amber Palaces'
RJ, XII–XIII (1972–73) 59-62

JONES, C. R. 314
'Dhuli–Citra : Historical Perspective on Art and Ritual'
in 'Kaladarsana' (*American Studies in the Art of India*) (*American Institute of Indian Studies, New Delhi 1981*) 69–75, 10 pls
With reference to wall-paintings (with powder) of 17th century in Kerala.

JOSHI, M. C. 315
'Siva Temple at Rajamau and the Historical Paintings of 1857 Revolt'
MADHU (M. N. Deshpande Fel. Vol. Delhi 1981) 273–74
In Rae-Bareli district, Uttar Pradesh.

KANG. KANWARJIT 316
'Album of Wall Paintings'
MARG, XXX-4 (Sept 1977) 69–76, 19 pls (4 colour)
Wall paintings of the so-called Chhatri of Bharmal, Ganesh Pol and palaces of Amer, Bairath, Galta and other places near Jaipur.

KIPLING, J. S. 317
'(The) Mosque of Wazir Khan Lahore'
Journal of Indian Art London, II (1887) 17-18, 5 coloured pls
Deals with mural paintings of the Mosque, typically Mughal of the 17th century.

MITTAL, JAGDISH 318
'Mural Painting in Chamba'
JISOA, XIX (1952-53) 11–18

MITTAL. JAGDISH 319
'(The) Wall Paintings of Chamba'
MARG, VIII-3 (June 1955) 38–42 and 7 pls

NAGPALL. J. C. 320
'Analysis of Some Moghul Wall Painting Materials'
Science and Culture, XX (1964) 122-25

NATH, R.   321
'Depiction of Animate Motifs at the Tomb of Itmad'ud-Daulah at Agra'
IsC, XLVII-4 (Oct 1973) 289-300, 19 pls
Based on a study of mural and miniature paintings; also examines the lawfulness of painting in Muslim art; important information of Mughal painting of Jehangir's time.

NATH, R.   322
'Incised Painting in Mughal Architecture'
QRHS, IX-3 (1969-70) 134-36
Mural stylized paintings from the tomb of Akbar to the Taj Mahal at Agra; particularly deals with pigments and process.

NATH, R   323
'Mughal Hammam and the Institution of Ghusal-Khāna'
IsC, XLIV-2 (April 1970) 101-10, 3 figs
References to mural stylized and other ornamental paintings of Hammams of Fatehpur Sikri.

NATH, R.   324
'Tomb of Md. Ghauth at Gwalior'
SI, XI-1 (Jan 1978) 21-30, 8 pls
Refers to mural paintings of the Tomb, built during Akbar's reign.

NEERAJ, JAISINGH   325
'Alwar-ke-Bhitti-Chitra' (Hindi)
RJ, XII-XIII (1972-73) 39-42
Mural paintings of Alwar.

PARMAR, B. M. S.   326
'Bundi-Tonk ke Bhitti-Chitra' (Hindi)
SP, XXVI-2 (April-June 1975) 66-71
Mural paintings of Bundi, Dugari, Tonk, Uniara, Nagar etc, 17th to 19th century.

PARMAR, B M. S.   327
'Nagar-ke-Bhitti Chitra' (Hindi)
SP, XXVII-3 (July-Sept 1976) 18-22
Mural painting of Nagar near Tonk 18th century.

PARMAR, B. M. S.   328
'Uniara-ke-Bhitti Chitra' (Hindi)
SP, XXVII-1 (Jan-March 1976) 33-41
Mural paintings of Uniara in Tonk 18th-19th century.

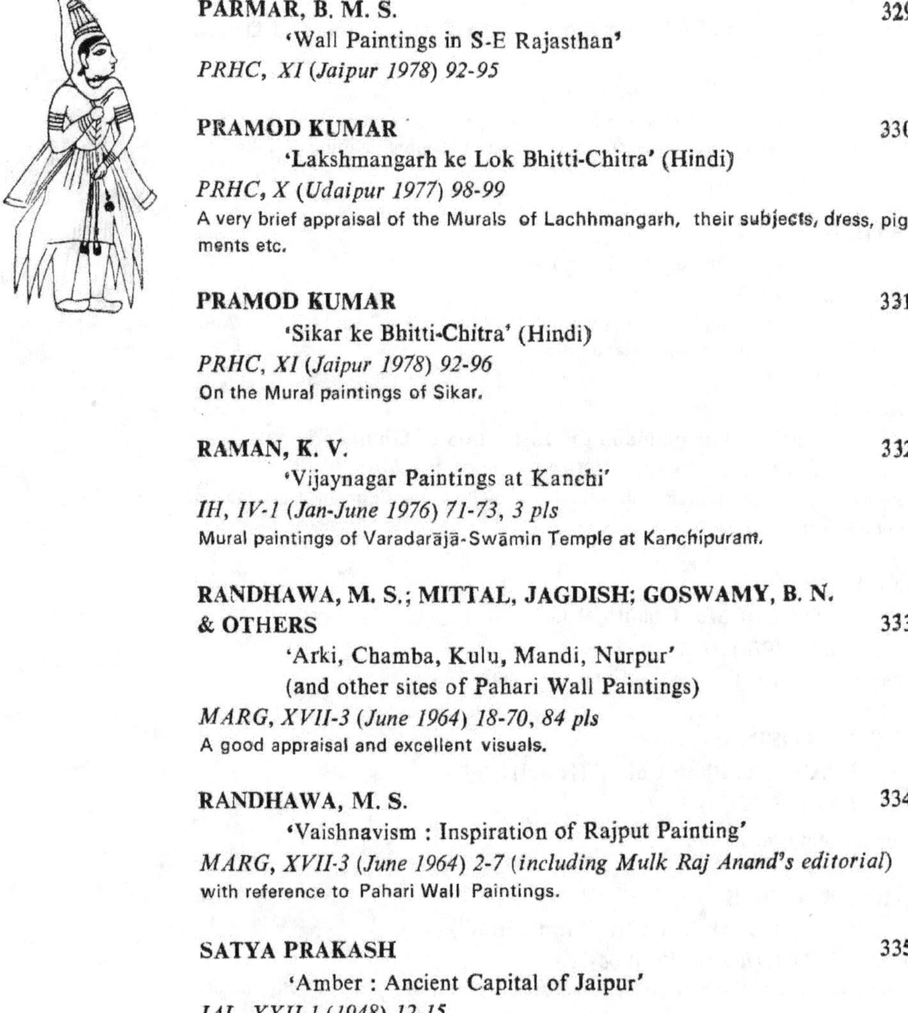

PARMAR, B. M. S.   329
'Wall Paintings in S-E Rajasthan'
PRHC, XI (Jaipur 1978) 92-95

PRAMOD KUMAR   330
'Lakshmangarh ke Lok Bhitti-Chitra' (Hindi)
PRHC, X (Udaipur 1977) 98-99
A very brief appraisal of the Murals of Lachhmangarh, their subjects, dress, pigments etc.

PRAMOD KUMAR   331
'Sikar ke Bhitti-Chitra' (Hindi)
PRHC, XI (Jaipur 1978) 92-96
On the Mural paintings of Sikar.

RAMAN, K. V.   332
'Vijaynagar Paintings at Kanchi'
IH, IV-1 (Jan-June 1976) 71-73, 3 pls
Mural paintings of Varadarāja-Swāmin Temple at Kanchipuram.

RANDHAWA, M. S.; MITTAL, JAGDISH; GOSWAMY, B. N.
& OTHERS   333
'Arki, Chamba, Kulu, Mandi, Nurpur'
(and other sites of Pahari Wall Paintings)
MARG, XVII-3 (June 1964) 18-70, 84 pls
A good appraisal and excellent visuals.

RANDHAWA, M. S.   334
'Vaishnavism : Inspiration of Rajput Painting'
MARG, XVII-3 (June 1964) 2-7 (including Mulk Raj Anand's editorial)
with reference to Pahari Wall Paintings.

SATYA PRAKASH   335
'Amber : Ancient Capital of Jaipur'
IAL, XXII-1 (1948) 12-15
Describes its palaces, temples and mural paintings.

SATYA PRAKASH   336
'(A) Note On Some Typical Jaipur Frescoes'
LK, 1-2 (April 1955-March 1956) 136-38, 11 pls
Of late 17th century A. D. at Amber and late 18th century at Galta; mythological scenes and Rāgamālās; he also deals with process and colours; a very useful article.

SATYA PRAKASH 337

'Rajasthan ki Bhitti-kala ki Paramparagat Chitra-Nirman-
Paddhatı' (Hindi)
RJ, V-VI (1964-65) 107-8
Traditional way of doing the Rajasthani mural painting; valuable article on its
technique and procedure.

SATYA PRAKASH 338

'Rajasthan men Chitrakala ka Kramik Vikas' (Hindi)
RB, VIII. 1-2 (March 1963) 9-19, 4 pls
Also deals with mural paintings of Amer, Chittor and Kumbhalgarh.

SATYA PRAKASH 339

'Wall-Paintings-Technique of their Execution and Preservation'
Journal of Indian Museums, XIII (1957)

SIVARAMAMURTI, C. 340

'Vijaynagar Painting from Lepakshi'
*Vijaynagar Sexcentenary Commemoration Volume Dharwar (1936;) also
see his* **Paintings from Lepakshi'** *JISOA, V (1937) 184-87*

SMITH, E. W. 341

'Akbar's Tomb at Sikandara' (Agra)
Journal of Indian Art London, VI (Nos. 46-53) (London 1896) 75-80
11 full-page illustrations (pls 30-40)
Also deals with its mural paintings (in the vestibule etc).

SMITH, E. W. 342

'Decorative Painting from the Tomb of Itmād' ud-Daulah
Agra'
Journal of Indian Art London VI (1895) 91-94, 8 colour pls

SMITH, E. W. 343

'Wall Paintings from the Jami' Masjid Fatehpur Sikri near
Agra'
Journal of Indian Art, VIII (1899) 55-57. 10 col. pls
Condensed from **Mughal Architecture of Fatehpur Sikri** Part—IV.

SMITH. E. W. 344

'Wall-Paintings from Salim Chishti's Tomb Fatehpur Sikri
near Agra'
Journal of Indian Art London VIII (1898) 41-44. 12 col. pls
Condensed from his **'Mughal Architecture of Fatehpur Sikri'** Part—III.

SMITH, E. W.   **345**

  'Wall-Paintings recently found in the Khwabgah, Fatehpur
   Sikri near Agra'

*Journal of Indian Art London VI (Nos. 46-53) (1896) pp. 65-68, 11 pls
(9 colour)*

SRIVASTAVA, R. P.   **346**

  'Inventory of Panjab Frescoes'

The Panjab Past and Present Patiala, XIII-1 (April 1979) 66-72

Gives a list of some 75 monuments where the mural paintings are extant. But
there is no date and no chronological arrangement. It appears that the List
mostly refers to 18th century and later works.

4

PALM-LEAF, SCROLL (Pata, Cloth) & PICHHAI PAINTINGS
(INCLUDING RUMALS, SHAWLS & OTHER PAINTED TEXTILES)

BOOKS

ANAND, MULK RAJ (ed.)   **347**
      'Treasures of Indian Textiles'
      (Calico Museum Ahmedabad)
(*Marg Publications Bombay 1980*)
Numerous mono and colour pls of superb quality and learned articles on painted textiles by Pupul Jayakar, Alfred Buhler, Anand Krishna, Kay Talwar and Kalyan Krishna and others.

BAKER, G. P.   **348**
      'Calico Painting and Printing in the East Indies in the XVIIth
      and XVIIIth Centuries'
(*London 1921*)

BHATTACHARJEE, A. K.   **349**
      'Chamba Rumal'
(*Indian Museum Calcutta 1969*) *pp. 89, 18 pls*

BHATTACHARYA, B.   **350**
      'Krishna in Traditional Painting of Bengal'
(*Calcutta 1972*) *pp. 59, 28 pls*
Historical Account of Paṭa painting of Bengal in modern times.

BRIJ BHUSHAN, JAMILA   **351**
      '(The) Costumes and Textiles of India'
(*Taraporevala Bombay 1958*)
Also deals with calicos, cloth printing and other allied subjects.

GEIJER, AGNES   352
  'Oriental Textiles in Sweden'
(*Rosenkilde & Bagger, Copenhagen*)
16th century and later textiles

GULATI, A. N.   353
  '(The) Patolu of Gujarat'
(*Museums Association of India Bombay*)

IRWIN, JOHN & BRETT, K. B.   354
  'Origins of Chintz'
(*London 1970*)
With a catalogue of Indo-European cotton paintings in the Victoria and Albert Museum London etc; an excellent work on post-Medieval cotton paintings of South India; Reviewed by Khandalavala in the **LK** No. 15 (1972) 67-68.

IRWIN, JOHN & HALL, M.   355
  'Indian Painted & Printed Fabrics'
(*London 1971*)

KAR, K. C. & Others   356
  'Ramayana in Ordisi Pata Painting'
(*Cuttack 1977*) *75 colour pls*

MOTICHANDRA   357
  'Costumes Textiles Cosmetics & Coiffure in Ancient &
    Medieval India'
(*Delhi 1973*)
Valuable references to painted cotton fabrics.

PUNYAVIJAYA, MUNI   358
  'Jaisalmer Chitravali' (Hindi)
(*Ahmedabad 1951*)

PUNYAVIJAYA, MUNI (ed)   359
  'Jaisalmer-ni Chitra-Samriddhi' (Gujarati)
(*Sarabhai M. Nawab, Ahmedabad, n. d*)
Palm-leaf Jaina paintings of 12th-13th centuries from Jaisalmer.

SHASTRI, HIRANAND   360
  'Ancient Vijnapatipatṛas'
(*Gaekward Coronation Com. No.1 Baroda 1942*) *ix+80, 29 pls*
Painted scrolls of the Jainas; also see Jinavijaya's 'Vijnapti-Ṭriveṇī'.

SKELTON, ROBERT   361
   'Rajasthani Temple Hangings of the Krishna Cult'
(*London, New York 1973*)
On Pichhwāis (painted wall hangings).

TALWAR, KAY & KALYAN KRISHNA   362
   'Indian Pigment Paintings on Cloth'
(*Ahmedabad 1979*) *also printed in the form of an article in*
Treasures of Indian Textiles (*Marg Bombay 1980*) *117–26 and pls*

TUCCI, G.   363
   'Tibetan Painted Scrolls'
(*Rome 1949)*

—   364

   'Indian Museum Calcutta : General Guide Book'
(*Indian Museum Calcutta 1959*) *& pls*
Catalogues contents of the Art Section of the Museum e. g. Temple banners,
scrolls, miniatures and textiles.

ARTICLES

AGRAWALA, V. S.   365
   'A Jaina Cloth Painting or Chitrapata of Taruna Prabha Suri'
Journal of the U. P. Historical Society XXII pp. 214–15

AHIVASI, DEVKI   366
   'Bharat Kala Bhavan men Sangrahit kesar se Chitrit ek Saree'
      (Hindi)
Chhavi (1971) 395-96, 5 pls of figures
From Gujarat of mid-19th century A. D.

ANAND, M. R.   367
   'Chamba Rumals'
MARG VII-4 (Sept 1954) 35-40, 4 pls (1 colour)
A beautiful Introduction to this branch of Textiles.

ANAND, M. R.   368
   'Homage to Kalamkari'
Marg XXXI-4 (Sept 1978) 2-18, 7 pls
With reference to the Painted cloths of India; it gives a good introduction.

ANDHARE, SHRIDHAR 369
'(A) Note on the Mahavira Samavasaraṇa Pata'
Chhavi (1971) 345–45 with pls

BANERJEE, P. 370
'An Illustrated Palm-Leaf Ms. of the Period of Jayarjunadeva
of Nepal'
LK No. 17 (n. d.) 22–28, 8 pls, 1 fig
Dated 1350 A. D.

BANERJI, ADRIS 371
'Phulkaris' (A Folk Art of the Punjab)
Marg VIII–3 (June 1955) 56–64, 14 pls
Popular art of textile.

BEACH, M. C. 372
'Rajasthani Temple Hangings of the Krishna Cult'
Oriental Art Oxford XX–3 (1974) 337–39, 3 pls
On pichhavājs.

BRETT, KATHARINE 373
'Some Important Indian Chintzes in the Royal Ontario
Museum Toronto'
Marg XXXI–4 (Sept 1978) 75–76, 2 pls
18th-19th century painted and printed cloths.

BRETT, M. K. 374
'Indian Painted and Dyed Cottons for the European Market'
*In '**Aspects of Indian Art**' (ed. P. Pal, Brill Leiden 1972) 167–71, 10 pls*
Beginning from the 17th century A. D.

BUHLER, ALFRED 375
'Indian Resist–Dye Fabrics'
*In '**Treasures of Indian Textiles**' (Marg Bombay 1980) 97–110 & pls*
Painted cotton and silk textiles from Rajasthan, Gujarat and other states.

CHATTERJEE, S. K. 376
'An Old Hindu Painting on Cloth from the Island of Bali'
Year-Book of the Asiatic Society of Bengal (1937) III. 153–55

DANE, LANCE 377
'(The) Romance of Indo European Textile Trade'
In **'Treasures of Indian Textiles'** (*Marg Bombay 1980*) *81–96 & pls*
Deals with painted chintz and other Indian textiles exported to Europe 17th-19th centuries; a summary of John Irwin's **'Studies in Indo-European Textile History'** (Calico Museum of Textiles Ahmedebad).

DALMIA, Y. 378
'Kalamkari'
Marg XXX-4 (Sept 1978) 81–83 and pls
Notes on painted cotton

DAS, J. P. 379
'Patachiṭra of Orissa'
Marg XXXI-4 (Sept 1978) 65, 1 colour pl.
Painted scrolls.

DAVE, S. K. 380
'Okha-Mandal Pradesh-man Chitra, Shilpa ane Sthapatya-Kala
(Accho-Parichaya) (Gujarati)
SB XI-3 (April 1974) 204–17
Painting Sculpture and Architecture in Okha-Mandala (Saurashtra), deals with painted textiles and wall-paintings also.

DHAMIJA, J. 381
'(The) Pichhwais of Nathdwara'
Times of India Annual (1965) 73–80 & pls

DOSHI, SARYU 382
'Dazzling to the Eye : Picchhavais from the Deccan'
Marg XXXI-4 (Sept 1978) 55–60, 3 colour pls

DOSHI, SARYU 383
'Spring Feeling : The Vasanta Vilasa' (Three Vignettes)
Marg XXXI-4 (Sept 1978) 37–38, 3 pls
Three Vasant-Vilāsa paintings on scroll dated 1451 A. D. Ahmedabad.

DOSHI, SARYU & ANDHARE, SHRIDHAR 384
'Painted Banners on Cloth :
(1) Vivadha Tīrtha-Pata of Ahmedabad
(2) The Panch Kalyāṇaka-Pata, School of Aurangadad'
Marg XXXI-4 (Sept 1978) 40–54, 12 pls (8 excellent full-page colour)
Reference to Vijnaptipatṛas and other painted cloth scrolls; the former is dated 1641 A. D.

FISCHER, E & Others   385
'Matano Candarvo' (Gujarati)
(Textile pieces for Goddess Worship in Gujarat)
Marg XXXI-4 (Sept 1978) 61-64, 2 colour pls

GANGOLY, O. C.   386
'A Group of Vallabhacharya or Nathdwara Paintings and
Their Relatives'
BMB I-2 (1944) 31-40 & pls

GANGULI, K. K.   387
'Chamba Rumal'
JISOA XI (1943) 69-74

GHOSE, AJIT   388
'·Miniatures of a Newly discovered Buddhist Palm-Leaf Ms.
from Bengal'
AIOC. V-2 (Lahore 1928) 1071-80: also published in
RUPAM No. 38-39 (April-July 1929) 78-84 with notes

GHOSE, AJIT   389
'Old Bengal Paintings'
IAL II. 1-2 (1926) 20-40
A very useful enumeration of Pata drawings.

GOETZ, H.   390
'An Early Basohli- Chamba Rumal'
BMB III-1 (1945-46) 35-42 & pls; reprinted in the RAA 189-96 and pls

GOETZ, H.   391
'Notes on the Vallabhacharya Paintings from Udaipur and
Jodhpur in the Baroda Museum'
BMB I-2 (1944) 41-46 & pls

GOPAL, SURENDRA   392
'Social Life in Gujarat and Rajasthan in the 19th century'
(as revealed in a scroll of invitation)
JJC VI-3 (Jan 1972) 106-8, 5 pls
Vijnaptipatra sent from Merta to a Muni in A. D. 1810 containing beautiful
paintings on cloth.

HALDAR, ASIT KUMAR   393
   'Bengal ka Pata Chitra' (Hindi)
Kala Nidhi Banares 1-4 with pls
On Bengali Paṭa painting; the author holds the view that this folk art developed
from medieval Indian Painting.

HIDAYAT HUSAIN, M.   394
   'A Persian Stencilled Wall-hanging Picture said to represent
   'Umar Khayyam'
Year-book of the Asiatic Society of Bengal (1937) 159-61

IRWIN, JOHN   395
   'Golconda Cotton Paintings of the Early 17th century'
LK No 5 (April 1959) 11-48, 29 excellent pls (2 colour)
A very useful monograph dealing with cotton paintings of 1630-40 and 1640-50
period mainly based on travellers accounts.

IRWIN, JOHN   396
   '(The) Kashmir Shawl'
Marg VI-1 (Dec 1952) 43-50, 11 pls
of 17th—19th centuries.

IRWIN, JOHN   397
   '(The) Kashmir Shawl : Origin and Technique'
Marg VIII-2 (March 1955) 121-38. 21 pls 8 figs
Of 18th century and the later period; an excellent article.

IRWIN, JOHN   398
   '(The) Mogul Gallery : At the Victoria & Albert Museum'
Marg VII-1 (Dec 1953) 23-26, 4 pls
Includes references to a few Mughal textiles.

IRWIN, JOHN   399
   '(The) Significance of Chintz'
Marg XXXI-4 (Sept 1978) 67-74, 6 pls (4 excellent colour)
19th Century Painted and printed cloth for European market.

JAIN. PREM SUMAN   400
   'Pata-Chitravali ki Loka-Parampara' (Hindi)
RB Combined No. XII-XIII (1970) 219-35
An excellent article on cloth painting, its history and tradition, subjects etc.

JAYAKAR, PUPUL   401
   'Cotton Prints of Gujerat & Kathiawar'
Marg IV-4 (July 1950) 40-43, 6 sketches
Of 18th—19th centuries.

JAYAKAR, PUPUL 402
    'Gaiety in Colour & Form : Painted and Printed Cloths'
Marg XXXI-4 (Sept 1978) 23-36, 18 pls (6 excellent colour)

JAYAKAR, PUPUL 403
    'Indian Textiles through the Centuries'
In **'Treasures of Indian Textiles'** (*Marg Bombay 1980) 59-80, numerous pls*
A detailed and very useful survey of painted textiles.

JAYAKAR, PUPUL 404
    '(A) Seventeenth Century Satin Tissue Wall-Hanging from
       Ahmedabad'
LK 1-2 (April 1955-March 1956) 108-112, 2 pls
(1 colour) 1 fig

JAYAKAR, PREMLATA 405
    'Tie Dyed Fabrics of India'
Marg II-1 (October 1947) 93-102, 12 pls (3 colour)
Pāṭolā of Patan. Bandhanī (Chūnarī) and Balūchar Būṭedär etc.

KALYAN KRISHNA 406
    "Pichhvais-Temple Hangings of the Vallabhacharya Sect'
Indian Museums XXX (1974-75) 75-78 & pls

LOWRY, J. 407
    'Tibet, Nepal or China ? An Early Group of Dated Tangkas'
Oriental Art Oxford XIX-3 (1973) 306-15, 12 pls
15th century Buddhist Painted scrolls.

MANJESHWAR, NANDU 408
    'Thangkas : Tibet's Exquisite Scrolls'
Sunday Standard Magazine, May 31, 1981, p. 3
A very interesting article dealing with their genesis, method of painting,
classification etc.

MEHTA, N. C. 409
    'A Picture Roll from Gujarat' (A. D 1433)
Indian Art & Letters, VI (New Series) 71-78

MEHTA, R. N. 410
    'Picchavais : Temple Hangings of the Vallabhacharya Sect'
Journal of Indian Textile and Handicrafts, III (1957) 4-14

MEHTA, R. N.   **411**
'(A) Set of Decorative Textile of the Pushtimargiya Vaishnavas
in the Collection of the Baroda Museum'
BMB XIV (1962) 19-22

MISHRA, V.   **412**
'Paintings on Mica Sheets c.150 B. C.—A. D. 100'
LK 9 (April 1961) 58-59, 1 pl
7 Circular sheets out of 21 excavated near Patna bear very interesting paintings.

MOHAPATRA, R. P.   **413**
'Two Pata Paintings on Jagannath in Orissa State Museum'
The Orissa Historical Research Journal XIII-4 (1965) 43-48 & pls

MORLEY, GRACE (ed)   **414**
'(Pictorial Review of) Painted Temple Hangings from South
India'
NMB No. 1 (1966) p. 13, 11 pls on pp. 14 & 16-23;
Of 18th—19th centuries, exquisite workmanship.

MORLEY, GRACE (ed)   **415**
'(Pictorial Review of) Painted Wooden Doors from Mewar and
Marwar (19th century)'
NMB No. 1 (1966) 5 pls on pp. 11-12 & p. 15
In the mural style.

MORLEY, GRACE (ed)   **416**
'(Pictorial Review of) Palm-Leaf Ms. of the Bhojadeva-
Sangraha (A. D. 1189)'
NMB No. 1 (1966) 2 pls on p. 5;
The ms. has 6 paintings in Pāla-Nepal style.

MOTICHANDRA & DOSHI, SARYU   **417**
'Costumes through the Ages'
In **'Treasures of Indian Textiles'** *(Marg Bombay 1980) 19-58, numerous
text figures & colour pls*
Deals with painted textiles and their history; a very useful article.

NAHTA, AGARCHAND   **418**
'Jaina Chitrakala ki ek vishishta upalabdhi :
Sachitra Vijnapti-patra' (Hindi)
TP I-1 (Jan-March 1975) 22-25
On painted Jaina scrolls; a very informative article.

NAHTA, AGARCHAND 419

'Mewar ke Aghat-Durg men S. 1317 men chitrit Tadpatriya Jaina prati (Hindi)

SP V-3 (March 1954) 46-48

Palm-Leaf Jaina ms. of 1260 A. D. bearing paintings from Mewar.

NAHTA, AGARCHAND & NAHTA, BHANWARLAL 420

'Udaipur ka Sachitra Vijnapti-Patra' (Hindi)

NPP, LVII. 2-3 (V. S. 2009) 221-30, 4 pls

Painted scroll of Udaipur dated V. S. 1887/1830 A. D. with Jaina subjects; reference also to other scrolls from V. S. 1431 to V. S. 1916; a very useful and learned article.

NAHTA, BHANWARLAL 421

'Bikaner ka Sachitra Vijnapti-Patra' (Hindi)

RB I-4 (January 1947) 28-34

Painted scroll (Pata) 97 feet long and 11 inches broad dated V. S. 1898/1841 A. D. sent from Bikaner to Jaina Muni Jina Saubhagya Suriji containing beautiful figurative and decorative paintings; Jaina subjects are depicted on first 20 feet and natural scenes auspicious and religious things on 11.5 feet; scenes from the Bikaner city on 55 feet; then is the Vijnapti in Sanskrit; All this is something very interesting and historically useful.

NAHTA, BHANWARLAL 422

'Merta se Vijay-Jinendra Suri ko Virampur praishit Sachitra Vijnaptipatra' (Hindi)

Shri Mahabir Jaina Vidyalaya **Golden Jubilee Volume** *(Bombay 1968) 49-64, 4 pls*

32 feet long scroll (17' of which has paintings) sent from Merta to Virampur dated V. S. 1867/1810 A. D. showing Jaina subjects.

NAHTA, BHANWARLAL 423

Vijnaptipatra of Udaipur'

JJC, VII-1 (July 1972) 9-18, 5 figures

70 feet long scroll dated 1831A.D. from Udaipur to Bikaner containing paintings; the article also has useful references to other vijnaptipatras from 15th century onwards.

PAL, PRATAPADITYA 424

'Paintings from Nepal in the Prince of Wales Museum'

BPOW No. 10 (1967) 1-26, 28 pls

Scrolls (patas) from 14th century to 1821 A. D. Buddhist, Śaiva and Vaiṣṇava.

PANNALAL   425

'Prachin Patra' (Hindi)
JSB XIV-1 (July 1947) 24-27
Painted scroll 17' X 2' dated V. S. 1716/1659 A. D. written at Dhamoni near
(Sagar) with Jaina subjects.

PURAN SINGH   426

'Some Rumals from Chamba'
Rupam No. 32 (1927) 133-34
Bearing paintings.

SARASWATI, S. K.   427

'On An Illustrated Ms. of the Devimahatmya (Chandi) in the
form of a Miniature Scroll'
Year Book of the Asiatic Society of Bengal (1950) XVI-175

SATYA PRAKASH   427—A

'Calico-Printing of Jaipur'
Journal of Indian Museums Bombay X (1954) 33-35

SCHWARTZ, P. R.   428

'French Documents on Indian Cotton Painting'
*Journal of Indian Textile History, No. II (1956) 5-23; the second part of
the article was published in No. III of this Journal (1957) 15-44*
A very Interesting and learned article.

SHAH, U. P.   429

'Vardhamana-Vidya-Pata'
JISOA VI (1941) 42-51

SHASTRI, HIRANAND   430

'A Pre-Mughal Chitra-Pata from Gujarat'
IHQ XIV-3 (1938) 425-31

TALWAR, KAY & KALYAN KRISHNA   431

'Indian Pigment Paintings on Cloth'
In **'Treasures of Indian Textiles'** (*Marg Bombay 1980*) *117-26* &
numerous pls
Pichhāis, Jaina Paṭas, phaḍas of Rajasthan etc., A very useful article.

TANDON, B. N. 432
'(Chemical Analysis etc of) The Cloth Paintings of the 14th
and 15th centuries'
NMB No. 2 (1970) 32–36, 2 pls
Śatrunjaya Paṭa 14th century from Palitana and Saraswatī Paṭa 15th century
from Western India.

VARADARAJAN, LOTIKA 433
'Towards a Definition of Kalamkari'
Marg XXXI-4 (Sept 1978) 19–21
On cloth painting.

5

MINIATURE PAINTING :
(A) Buddhist, Nepalese and Eastern Indian

BOOKS

CHOWDHURY, P. C. (ed)   434
     'Hasti–Vidyārṇava'
(Publication Board Assam, Gauhati 1976) 171 colour pls
Mainly on elephant science; the miniatures were painted in 1734 A. D. under the
Ahom King Siva Simha.

DAS GUPTA, R.   435
     'Eastern Indian Manuscript Painting'
(Taraporevala Bombay) 100 pls (10 colour) and 10 figs

GUPTA, R. D.   436
     'Nepalese Miniatures'
(Varanasi 1968) with pls & figs
A good appraisal of the subject.

KRAMRISCH. STELLA   437
     '(The) Art of Nepal'
(New York 1964)

MADANJEET SINGH   438
     'Himalayan Art'
(Unesco London 1968)

PAL, PRATAPADITYA   439
   'Art of Tibet'
(*New York 1969*)

SECKEL, DIETRICH   440
   '(The) Art of Buddhism'
(*London 1964*)

ARTICLES

BANERJEE, P.   441
   'An Illustrated Ashta-Sahasrika Prajnaparmita Ms. in the
     Collection of the National Museum New Delhi'
LK No. 16 (1974) 33-36, 9 pls
Buddhist miniature painting of 12th century A. D. of Eastern India.

BANERJI, ADRIS   442
   'Art of the Eighteenth Century Bengal'
QRHS XIV-2 (1974-75) 96-105

BHATTACHARYYA, A. K.   443
   'A Dated Pancharaksha Ms. of the Reign of Govinda
     Pala Deva'
IMB IV-1 (Jan 1969) 114-16

BHATTACHARYA, B.   444
   'Twenty-two Buddhist Miniatures from Bengal (11th century)'
BMB I-1 (Aug 1943-June 1944) 17-36
A very learned and useful article on the subject.

DAS GUPTA, R.   445
   'Buddhist Paintings in Assam'
JISOA New Series Vol. VII (1975-76) 52-61

DAS GUPTA, R.   446
   'Painting in Assam, Tai Ahom'
AIOC XXII (Gauhati 1965) 191-93

DUTT, G. S.   447
   '(The) Indigenous Painters of Bengal'
JISOA I (1933) 18-25

GHOSH, D. P.   448
    'Eastern School of Medieval Indian Painting'
Chhavi (1971) 91–103 with pls
very useful article which deals both with manuscript painting and patas; his article : 'Orissan Painting' **JISOA** IX (1941) 194-200 may also be referred to on this subject.

GHOSH, M. R.   449
    '(A) Study of Tibetan Paintings at the Patna Museum'
AIOC VII (Baroda 1933) 784–90

KRAMRISCH, STELLA   450
    'Nepalese Paintings'
JISOA I (1933) 129–47
A very learned and indispensable article on the subject.

MOOKERJEE, MONOTOSH   451
    'An Illustrated Cover of a Manuscript of the Ashtasahasrikā
    Prajnā-Pāramitā in a Private Collection'
LK No. 6 (April 1959) 53–62, 3 colour pls
The ms. is dated 1028 A. D.; with Buddhist subjects.

MOTICHANDRA   452
    'A Pair of Painted Wooden Covers of the Karaṇḍavyūha Ms.
    Dated A. D. 1455 from Eastern India'
Chhavi (1971) 240–42 with pls

MOTICHANDRA   453
    'Two Illustrated Devīmahātmya Mss. from Nepal'
BPOW No. 11 (1971) 1–12, 12 pls
c. 1400 A. D., very interesting article.

PAL, PRATAPADITYA   454
    'Evidences of Buddhist Painting in Eastern India in the 15th
    century'
JAS 4th Series VIII–4 (1966) 267–70 with pls

SANKRITYAYANA, RAHUL   455
    'Buddhist Painting in Tibet' and 'Technique in Tibetan Painting'
Marg XVI–4 (Sept 1963) 17–37, 19 pls (2 colour)

SARASWATI, S. K.   **456**
    'East Indian Manuscript Painting'
Chhavi (1971) 243-62 with pls
c. 750-1150 of Pāla rulers of Bengal and Bihar; also gives a list of mss. of East
Indian style of Painting; a very learned and useful article.

SHARMA, S. M.   **457**
    'Miniature Paintings in Assam'
AIOC XIX (Delhi 1957) 160-61

VATSYAYAN, KAPILA   **458**
    '(The) Illustrated Manuscripts of the Gita–Govinda from
      Orissa'
Madhu (M. N. Deshpande Fel. Vol. Delhi 1981) 275-86, 11 pls
16th to 19th century; a very learned article.

MINIATURE PAINTING
(B) Medieval Loka-Kala

(Jaina, Apabhramsa, Rajasthani and Gujarati
so called Western Indian;
Malwa, Jaunpur and the Deccan—
Indigenous Styles of the Medieval Period 11th-17th Centuries A.D.)

5

BOOKS

ANAND KRISHNA   459
    'Malwa Painting'
(*Varanasi 1963*)
A scholarly treatise of great use.

ARCHER, W. G.   460
    'Central Indian Painting'
    (with Introduction and Notes)
(*Faber & Faber London 1958*) *10 colour pls*
Reviewed in the **LK** No. 7 (April 1960) 91; good work on the subject.

BROWN, W. NORMAN   461
    '(A) Descriptive and Illustrated Catalogue Of Miniature
        Paintings of the Jaina Kalpa Sutra'
(*Freer Gallery of Art Washington, 1934*) *iv + 66, 54 pls*

BROWN, W. NORMAN   462
    'India and Indology'
    (Selected articles ed. by Rosane Rocher)
(*Moti Banarsi Delhi 1978*)
Its Part—III deals with Brown's eight articles on Western Indian or Jaina Painting.

BROWN, W. NORMAN   463

'(The) Mahimnastava or Praise of Shiva's Greatness'
(*AIIS Poona 1965*)
39 Miniature paintings of early 17th century of the indigenous style.

BROWN, W. NORMAN   464

'Manuscript Illustration of the Uttaradhyayana Sūtra'
(*American Oriental Society, New Haven 1941*)

BROWN, W. NORMAN   465

'(The) Saundarya–Laharī or Flood of Beauty'
(*Harvard Oriental Series, Cambridge Ms. 1958*)
With illustrations of miniature painting of medieval indigenous style.

BROWN, W. NORMAN   466

'(The) Story of Kālaka'
(*Freer Gallery of Art, Washington 1933*) *vii+149; 15 pls*
On the miniature paintings of (Jaina) Kālakāchārya Kathā

COOMARASWAMY, A. K.   467

'Catalogue of Jaina Paintings and Manuscripts'
(*Boston 1924*)

KHANDALAVALA, KARL J. & MOTICHANDRA   468

'An Illustrated Āranyaka Parvan in the Asiatic Society of
   Bombay'
(*The Asiatic Society Bombay 1974*) *pp. 53, 64 pls (8 colour)*
Reviewed in the LK No. 18, 45-46; the ms. is dated 1516 A. D.; the learned
authors discuss Laur-Chanda and Chaur-Panchāshikā groups (Jaunpur Mandu
etc) of 15th and early 16th century A. D. An excellent treatise for study of the
Pre-Mughal miniature Painting.

KHANDALAVALA, KARL J.   469

'Gita-Govind'
(*New Delhi 1968*) *10 pls*

KHANDALAVALA, KARL J ; MOTICHANDRA &   470
PRAMODCHANDRA

'Miniature Paintings from Sri Motichand Khajanchi Collection'
(*Lalit Kala Akademi New Delhi 1960*)

KHANDALAVALA, KARL J. & MOTICHANDRA   471
'New Documents of Indian Painting : A Reappraisal'
(*Bombay 1969*)
Reviewed by Douglas Barrett in the **LK** No. 15 (1972) 57-58; a very learned and useful work on pre-Mughal indigenous styles of miniature painting

MAJUMDAR, M. R.   472
'A 15th Century Gita-Govinda Ms. with Gujarati Paintings'
(*Bombay 1938*)

MEHTA, N. C.   473
'Gujarati Painting in the 15th century'
(*The Indian Society, London 1913*) *16 pls*
On Vasantavilāsa paintings

MOTICHANDRA   474
'Jaina Miniature Paintings from Western India'
(*Ahmedabad 1949*)

MOTICHANDRA   475
'Studies in Early Indian Painting'
(*Bombay 1974*)

MOTICHANDRA (ed.)   476
'Seminar on Indian Art History'
(*Lalit Kala Akademi New Delhi 1962*)
The Greatest and most momentous seminar on Art held at Bharat Kala Bhawan Varanasi March 11-13, 1961. The greatest art critics and art historians like V. S. Agarwal, Motichandra, Niharranjan Ray, Rai Krishnadas, J. N. Banerjee, Karl J. Khandalavala, Pramodchandra, S. K. Saraswati etc participated. The third day session was held on 'Pre-Mughal Painting of the Sultanate period' (pp. 67-72). This style different from the western Indian style also existed; some very learned and useful discussions

MOTICHANDRA & SHAH, U. P.   477
'New Document of Jaina Painting'
(*Bombay 1975*) *pp. 103, 17 pls & 91 figs*
Reviewed in the **JJC** X-4 (April 1976) 161-62

NAWAB, SARABHAI M.   478
'Chitramaya Sri Pal Rasa'
(*Ahmedabad 1961*) *217 pls*
On medieval miniature painting style

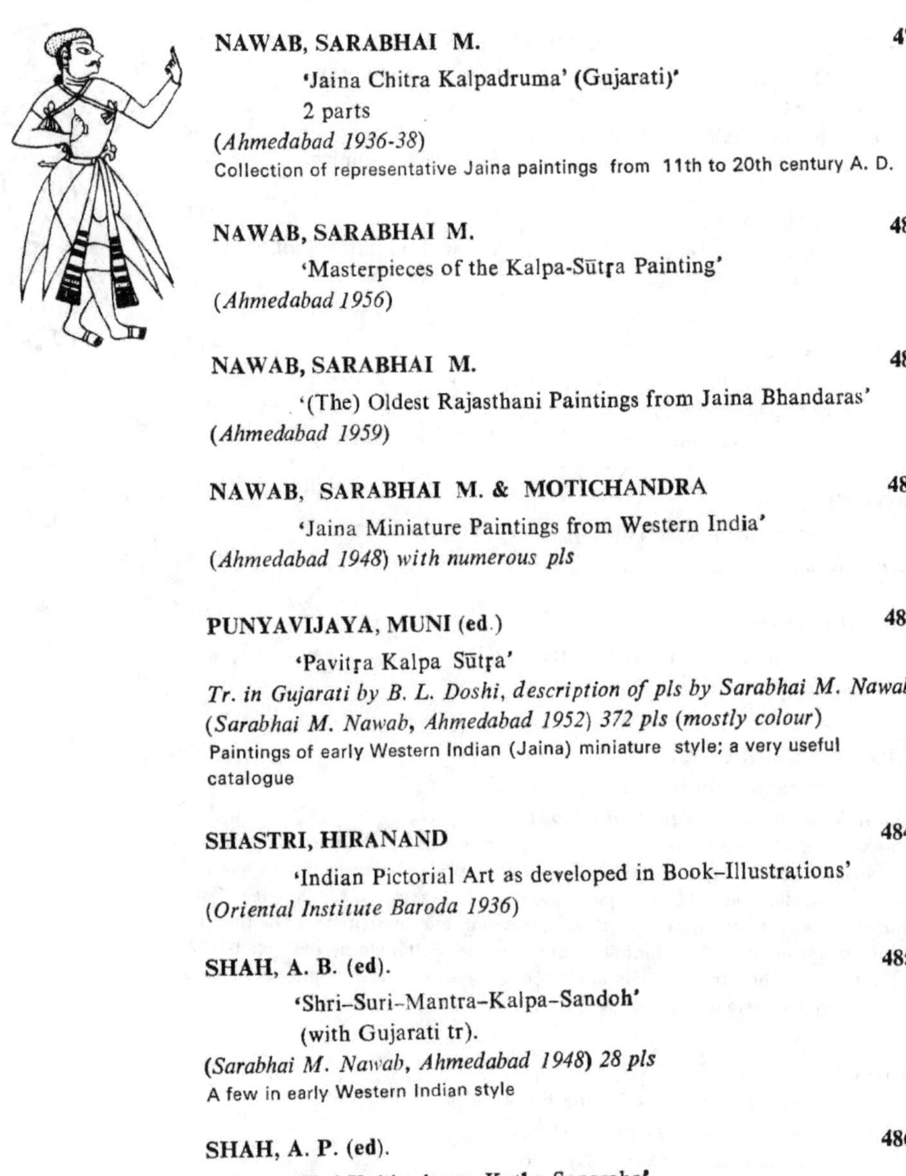

NAWAB, SARABHAI M. 479

'Jaina Chitra Kalpadruma' (Gujarati)'
2 parts
(*Ahmedabad 1936-38*)
Collection of representative Jaina paintings from 11th to 20th century A. D.

NAWAB, SARABHAI M. 480

'Masterpieces of the Kalpa-Sūtra Painting'
(*Ahmedabad 1956*)

NAWAB, SARABHAI M. 481

'(The) Oldest Rajasthani Paintings from Jaina Bhandaras'
(*Ahmedabad 1959*)

NAWAB, SARABHAI M. & MOTICHANDRA 482

'Jaina Miniature Paintings from Western India'
(*Ahmedabad 1948*) *with numerous pls*

PUNYAVIJAYA, MUNI (ed.) 483

'Pavitra Kalpa Sūtra'
Tr. in Gujarati by B. L. Doshi, description of pls by Sarabhai M. Nawab
(*Sarabhai M. Nawab, Ahmedabad 1952*) *372 pls (mostly colour)*
Paintings of early Western Indian (Jaina) miniature style; a very useful
catalogue

SHASTRI, HIRANAND 484

'Indian Pictorial Art as developed in Book–Illustrations'
(*Oriental Institute Baroda 1936*)

SHAH, A. B. (ed). 485

'Shri–Suri–Mantra–Kalpa–Sandoh'
(with Gujarati tr).
(*Sarabhai M. Nawab, Ahmedabad 1948*) *28 pls*
A few in early Western Indian style

SHAH, A. P. (ed). 486

'Shri Kalikacharya-Katha-Sangraha'
(Prakrat with Gujarati tr.)
(*Sarabhai M. Nawab, Ahmedabad 1949*) *88 pls (69 colour)*
14th century Miniature paintings of early Western Indian (Jaina) style

SHAH, U. P.   **487**
'More Documents of Jaina and Gujarati Paintings of 16th and
later Centuries'
(*L. D. Institute Ahmedabad 1976*)
Reviewed by Khandalavala in the **LK** No. 19 (1979) 70-71 and in the **JJC**
XIII-2 (October 1978) 81-83

SHAH, U. P.   **488**
'Studies in Jaina Art'
(*Varanasi 1955*)
Section on the Jaina Painting pp. 27-35

SHAH, U. P.   **489**
'Treasures of Jaina Bhandaras'
(*L. D. Institute Ahmedabad*) *9+100, 100 pls* (*18 colour*)
Wonderful catalogue of Illustrated Mss. of Jaina Bhandaras affording thorough
study of Jaina Painting; an indispensable work

SHIVESHWARKAR, LEELA   **490**
'(The) Pictures of the Chaura-Panchāshikā'
(A Sanskrit Love Lyric)
(*National Museum New Delhi 1967*) *18 colour pls*
On N. C. Mehta collection of Chaurapanchāshikā, 1540-70 A. D.

SPINK, WALTER M.   **491**
'Krishnamandala-A Devotional Theme in Indian Art'
(*The University of Michigan, Ann Arbor, Michigan 1971*)
Miniatures of the Krishna theme; reviewed by Khandalavala in the LK No. 16
(1974) 53-54

VATSYAYANA, KAPILA   **492**
'Miniatures of Gita-Govinda'
(*New Delhi*)

ARTICLES

ANAND KRISHNA   **493**
'Illustrated Leaves from a Pançatantṛa Ms. of the 15th century'
In '**Aspects of Jaina Art & Architecture**' (*Ahmedabad 1975*)
405-13 & 15 pls
So-called western Indian School of Painting

84

ANAND KRISHNA   494
'Krishna Lila Painting in the Baroda Museum'
BMB XX (1968) 11–18

ANAND KRISHNA   495
'Some Pre-Akbari Examples of Rajasthani Illustrations'
Marg XI–2 (March 1958) 18–19, 5 pls

ANAND KRISHNA   496
'Stylistic Study of Uttaradhyayan Sūtṛa Ms. 1591 A.D.'
BMB XV (1962) 1–12

ANDHARE, SHRIDHAR   497
'An Illustrated Ms. of Madhu-Mālatī Rī Chaupāī from
Lasani (Marwar)'
JISOA New Series VI (1974–75) 19–23

ANIS FAROOQI   498
'Indian Painting before Akbar'
JOR XXXIX (1969–70) 16–22, 3 pls
A very interesting and useful article

BENDER, ERNST   499
'A Gilt Illuminated Ms. of the Gita-Govinda'
JISOA New Series VI (1974–75) 24–26

BENDER, ERNST   500
'A Recent Acquisition : An Illustrated Ms. of
the Dhanna-Salibhadra-Chopai'
BMB XXV (1973-74) 1–8, 2 pls

BROWN, W. NORMAN   501
'A Jaina Ms. from Gujarat Illustrated in
Early Western Indian and Persian Styles'
*Ars Islamica Michigan, University of Michigan Com. Vol. IV (1937)
154–72, 12 pls*
Of early 16th century A. D.

BROWN, W. NORMAN   502
'Early Svetambara Miniature'
IAL III–1 (1929)

BROWN, W. NORMAN   503

      'Early Vaiṣṇava Miniature Paintings from Western India'
Eastern Art II (1930) 167–206 & pls
A very learned and useful survey

BROWN, W. NORMAN   504

      'Miniature Painting in Western India'
      (12th-17th century A. D.)
JJC IV-4 (April 1970) 199-213, 33 excellent pls
With reference to Jaina illustrated mss. He places them in two periods Palm-leaf
period (1127 to c. 1400) and Paper period (c. 1400 to 1650 A. D.); A very
interesting enumeration

BROWN, W. NORMAN   505

      'Stylistic Varieties of Early Western Indian Miniature Paintings
         about 1400 A. D.'
JISOA, V (1937) 2-12

CHANDRA KRISHNA, RAI   506

      'An Illustrated Leaves from a Pañcatantṛa Ms. of the 15th
         century'
In **'Aspects of Jaina Art & Architecture'** (*ed. U. P. Shah & M. A. Dhaky*)
(Ahmedabad 1975) 405-13

COOMARASWAMY, A. K.   507

      'Aesthetics and Relationship of Jaina Painting'
JJC IV-4 (April 1970) 214-17

COOMARASWAMY, A. K.   508

      'An Illustrated Jaina Manuscript'
Boston Museum's **Bulletin,** *Vol. XXXIII No. 197, 36-48*

COOMARASWAMY, A. K.   509

      'An Illustrated Svetambara Jaina Ms. of A. D. 1260'
Eastern Art Vol. II (Philadelphia 1930)

COOMARASWAMY, A. K.   510

      '(The) Conqueror's Life in Jaina Painting'
JISOA III (1935) 127-44

COOMARASWAMY, A. K. 511

'Notes on Jaina Art'
*Journal of Indian Art & Industry London, Vol. XVI No. 27 (July 1914)
81-97*

COOMARASWAMY, A. K. 512

'Two Western Indian Manuscripts'
Boston Museum's **Bulletin** *Vol. XXIX, 4-11*

DEVKAR, V. L. 513

'Some Recently Acquired Miniatures in the Baroda Museum'
BMB XII (1955-56) 19-24

DIGBY, SIMON 514

'(The) Literary Evidence for Painting in the Delhi Sultanate'
Bulletin of American Institute of Indian Studies Varanasi (1967)

DONALDSON, T. 515

'A Vijaya-Canda-Kevali-Charita Painting at Patan in A. D.
1499 in the Animated Style of the Vasanta-Vilasa'
JISOA New Series Dr Motichandra Com. Vol. (1978) 98-114

DOSHI, SARYU V. 516

'An Illustrated Ādipurāṇa of 1404 A. D. from Yoginipur
(Delhi)'
Chhavi (1971) 382-91 with pls
An important article

DOSHI, SARYU V, 517

'Twelfth Century Illustrated Ms. from Mudbidri'
BPOW No. 8 (1962-64) 29-36, 18 pls
Of the first quarter of the 12th century A. D. Jaina ms.

ETTINGHAUSEN, RICHARD 518

'(The) Bustan Ms. of Sultan Nāsir Shāh Khaljī'
Marg, XII-3 (June 1959) 42-43, 12 pls
Illustrated at Mandu c.1500-1510 A. D. gives a brief sketch only

GANGOLY, O. C.   519
    'An Editio Princeps of Sundara Śriṅgārā'
RUPAM No. 30 (April 1927) 47-50

GANGOLY, O. C.   520
    'Rajput Portraits of the Indigenous School'
Marg, VII-4 (Sept 1954) 12-21, 13 pls
A very learned and useful article

GANGOLY, O. C.   521
    'Three New Acquisitions of Indian Paintings'
BMB XII (1955-56) 15-18

GANGULI, K. K.   522
    'Late Medieval Painting in Western India : A Study'
JISOA Special No. (1965-66) 45-51
A general survey of Western Indian Art

GHOSE, AJIT   523
    'The Development of Jaina Painting'
AA II-3 (1927) 187-202, 2 pls; II-4 (1927) 278-82, 3 pls
The article is in two parts as above, on the origin and development of Jaina
Miniature Painting, very useful information; in Part-II he deals with Mughal and
Rajput influences

GHOSH, D. P.   524
    'An Illustrated Rāmāyaṇa Ms. of Tulsidas and Patas from
       Bengal'
JISOA XIII (1945) 130-38

GODE, P. K.   525
    'Illustrated Ms. of the Bhāgwata-Purāṇa copied in A. D. 1648'
New Indian Antiquary I (1938) 249-53

GOETZ, H.   526
    'Decline and Rebirth of Medieval Indian Art :
    Western Indian Painting'
Marg IV-2 (March 1951) 36-48, & pls

GOETZ, H.   527
    '(The) Laud Rāga Mālā Album and Early Rajput Painting'
JRAS (1954) 63-74 & 5 pls

GOETZ, H.   528

'(A) New Key to Early Rajput and Indo-Muslim Painting'
(A Unique Bhāgavata-Purāṇa, Daśama-Skandha, Album from
South-Western Marwar)

Roop-Lekha XXIII. 1-2 (1952) 1-16 & 3 pls; reprinted in **RAA** *(Wiesbaden 1978) 52-67, 10 pls*

Of late 16th century A. D.; interaction of various influences; a very useful analysis though many of his statements are to be taken with caution

GOETZ, H.   529

'Two Illustrations from the Sundara śṛṅgāra from Gujarat'
BMB VII (1949-50) 62-64

GORAKSHAKAR. S. V.   530

'A Dated Ms. of the Kālakāchārya Kathā in the Prince of
Wales Museum'
BPOW No. 9 (1964-66) 56-57, 3 pls
Dated 1366 A. D.

GOSWAMI, B. N. & DALLAPICCOLA, A. L.   531

'Leaves from a 17th century Ms. of the Devi-Mahatmya'
JISOA New Series, Dr Motichandra Com. Vol. (1978) 81-88
Very useful and interesting article

GRAY, BASIL   532

'Western Indian Painting in the 16th century :
The Origins of the Rajput School'
Burlington Magazine XC No. 539 (1948) 41-49

KHANDALAVALA, KARL J.   533

'A Gita-Govinda Series in the Prince of Wales Museum
(in the Style of Laur-Chandā and Chaura-Pancāśikā Group'
BPOW No. 4 (1953-54) 1-18 with pls
An indispensable article on the subject

KHANDALAVALA, KARL J.   534

'(The) Mrigavat of Bharat Kala Bhawan'
(as a Social Document and its Date and Provenance)
Chhavi (1971) 19-36 with numerous pls
Western Indian Style

KHANDALAVALA, KARL J.   535

'Problems of Rajasthani Painting' &
'The Origin and Development of Rajasthani Painting'
Marg XI-2 (March 1958) 4-17, 20 pls
Mainly on the indigenous Western Indian, so-called Rajasthani Painting

KHANDALAVALA, KARL J. & DOSHI, S.   536

'Miniature Paintings'
(On Pattas, Palm-Leaf and Paper)
In '**Jaina Art & Architecture**' (*Bharatiya Jnanpith New Delhi 1975*)
(*ed. by A. Ghosh*) *Vol, III 393-427, 40 mono and 28 colour pls*
An excellent authoritative monograph on Jaina Painting on cloth,
Palm-Leaf and Paper

KHANDALAVALA, KARL J. & MITTAL, JAGDISH   537

'(The) Bhāgavata Mss. from Palam and Isarda—
A Consideration in Style'
LK No. 16 (1974) 28-32, 4 pls
On a ms. of the Delhi-Agra region c. 1550-70 A. D.

KHANDALAVALA, KARL J. & MOTICHANDRA   538

'(A) Consideration of an Illustrated Ms. from Mandapadurga
(Mandu) Dated 1439 A. D.'
(and its bearing on Certain Problems of Indian Painting)
LK No. 6 (Oct 1959) 8-29, 27 pls and 3 colour pls. 1 fig.
Jaina ms; an excellent and most authoritative study of the subject;

KHANDALAVALA, KARL J. & MOTICHANDRA   539

'An Illustrated Kalpasūtra Painted at Jaunpur in A. D. 1465'
LK No. 12 (Oct 1962) 9-15, 20 pls (3 colour)
An extremely useful article

KHANDALAVALA, KARL J. & MOTICHANDRA   540

'An Illustrated Ms. of the Āraṇyaka Parvan in the Collection
of the Asiatic Society of Bombay'
Journal of the Asiatic Society of Bombay Vol. XXXVIII (1963-64)
116-21
15th century paintings of Gujarat

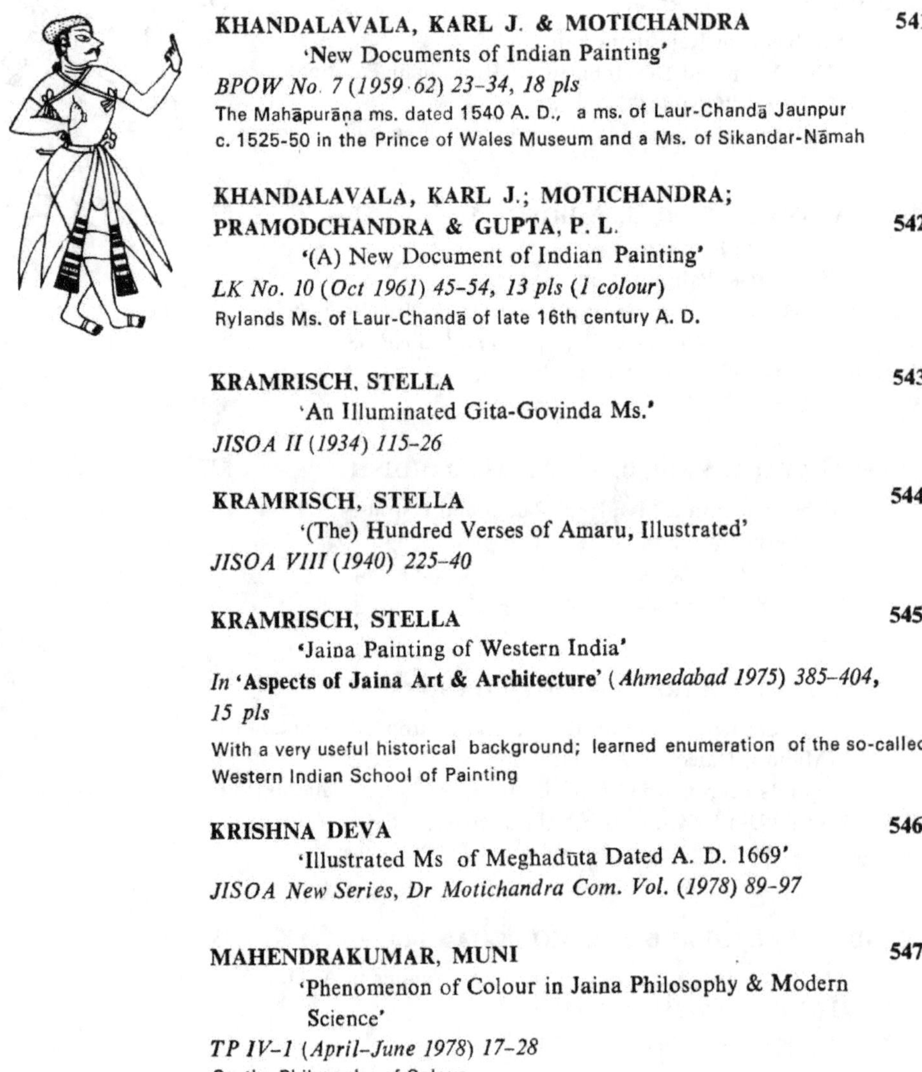

KHANDALAVALA, KARL J. & MOTICHANDRA   541
'New Documents of Indian Painting'
BPOW No. 7 (1959-62) 23-34, 18 pls
The Mahāpurāṇa ms. dated 1540 A. D., a ms. of Laur-Chandā Jaunpur
c. 1525-50 in the Prince of Wales Museum and a Ms. of Sikandar-Nāmah

KHANDALAVALA, KARL J.; MOTICHANDRA;
PRAMODCHANDRA & GUPTA, P. L.   542
'(A) New Document of Indian Painting'
LK No. 10 (Oct 1961) 45-54, 13 pls (1 colour)
Rylands Ms. of Laur-Chandā of late 16th century A. D.

KRAMRISCH, STELLA   543
'An Illuminated Gita-Govinda Ms.'
JISOA II (1934) 115-26

KRAMRISCH, STELLA   544
'(The) Hundred Verses of Amaru, Illustrated'
JISOA VIII (1940) 225-40

KRAMRISCH, STELLA   545
'Jaina Painting of Western India'
In **'Aspects of Jaina Art & Architecture'** *(Ahmedabad 1975) 385-404,*
15 pls

With a very useful historical background; learned enumeration of the so-called
Western Indian School of Painting

KRISHNA DEVA   546
'Illustrated Ms of Meghadūta Dated A. D. 1669'
JISOA New Series, Dr Motichandra Com. Vol. (1978) 89-97

MAHENDRAKUMAR, MUNI   547
'Phenomenon of Colour in Jaina Philosophy & Modern
    Science'
TP IV-1 (April-June 1978) 17-28
On the Philosophy of Colour

MAJUMDAR, M. R.   548
'A Dated Ms. of the Kākaruta-śāstṛa illustrated in the Western
    Indian Style'
LK No. 9 (April 1961) 55-56, 3 pls & 1 fig.
From Devas (Malwa) 1532 A. D.

MAJUMDAR, M. R.   **549**
    'Earliest Devī-Mahātmya Miniatures with Special Reference to Shakti-Worship in Gujarat'
JISOA VI (1938) 118–36

MAJUMDAR, M. R.   **550**
    '(The) Gujarati School of Painting and some Newly Discovered Vaiṣṇava Miniatures'
JISOA X (1942) 1–31
Very learned and useful article

MAJUMDAR, M. R.   **551**
    'Illustrated Mss. of Saundarya Lahirī and Śiva-Mahātmya Stotṛa in Early West Indian Style'
BMB IX (1952–53) 31–42

MAJUMDAR. M. R.   **552**
    'Illustrations of Śālihotṛa'
MB XIV (1962) 1–8

MAJUMDAR, M. R.   **553**
    'Newly Discovered Durgā-Pātha Miniatures of the Gujarati School of Painting'
New Indian Antiquary II (1939) 311–16, 1 pl

MAJUMDAR, M. R.   **554**
    '(A) Newly Discovered Illuminated Gita-Govind Ms. from Gujarat'
Journal of the University of Bombay X-2 (1974) 119–31

MAJUMDAR, M. R.   **555**
    '(A) Note on the Western Indian or Gujarati Miniatures in Baroda Art Gallery'
BMB II-2 (Feb-July 1945) 21-28

MAJUMDAR, M R.   **556**
    'Pashchimi Shaili men Balagopala-Stuti : Ek Aur Prati' (Hindi)
Poddar Abhinandana Grantha Mathura (1954) 763–73 & pls

MAJUMDAR. M. R.   **557**
    'Some Illustrated Mss. of the Gujarati School of Painting'
AIOC VII (1933) 827–35
Bāla Gopāla-Stuti, Bilva Mangala and Bhāgavata-Daśama-Skandha mss.

MAJUMDAR, M. R.   **558**

'Some Interesting Jaina Miniatures in the Baroda Art Gallery'
BMB IV (Aug 1946-July 1947) 27-32

MAJUMDAR, M. R.   **559**

'Specimens of Arts allied to Painting from Western India'
New Indian Antiquary I (1938) 377-82 & pls

MAJUMDAR, M. R.   **560**

'Two Illustrated Mss. in West Indian Style'
BMB XV (1962) 13-20

MAJUMDAR, M. R.   **561**

'Two Illustrated Mss. of the Bhāgavata Daśama-Skandha'
LK No. 8 (Oct 1960) 47-54, 11 pls (4 colour)
Dated 1611 and mid-17th century A. D.

MEHTA, N. C.   **562**

'Indian Painting in the 15th century :
An Early Illuminated Ms.'
Rupam Nos. 22-23 (1925)

MEHTA, N. C.   **563**

'(A) New Document of Gujarati Painting'
JISOA XIII (1945) 36-48;
Also see his 'A New Document of Gujarati Paintings : A Gujarati Version of the
Gita-Govinda' Journal of the Gujarat Research Society Ahmedabad VII-4 (1945)

MOTICHANDRA   **564**

'An Illustrated Ms. of Mahāpurāṇa in the Collecuon of Sri
Digambar Naya Mandir Delhi'
LK No. 5 (April 1959) 68-81, 9 pls (1 colour)
Late 15th century, Western Indian School, a very learned article

MOTICHANDRA   **565**

'An Illustrated Set of the Amaru-śataka'
BPOW No. 2 (1951-52) 1-63, with pls
An excellent monograph by one of the most competent authorities
on the subject

MOTICHANDRA	566
'An Illustrated Ms. of the Kalpa-Sūtṛa and Kālakāchārya-
Kathā'
BPOW No. 4 (1953-54) 40-48 with pls

MOTICHANDRA	567
Illustrated Ms. of Nala-Damayantī in the Prince of Wales
Museum Bombay'
ROOPLEKHA III-1 (1946) 20-21

MOTICHANDRA	568
'Pigments used in Jaina Miniatures'
JJC IV-4 (April 1970) 218-224

MOTICHANDRA & GUPTA P. L.	569
'An Illustrated Ms. of the Rasikapriyā'
BPOW No. 8 (1962-64) 18-21, 7 pls
c. 1666 A. D.

MOTICHANDRA & SHAH, U. P.	570
'New Documents of Jaina Paintings'
Shri Mahabir Jaina Vidyalaya **Golden Jubilee Volume**, *Part-1*
(Bombay 1968) 348-420, 50 pls (10 colour)
Very important and useful monograph; also published in book-form
(Bombay 1975)

NAHAR, P. S.	571
'An Illustrated Salibhadra Manuscript'
JISOA I (1933) 63-67; **JJC** *XI-1 (July 1976) 6-12, 5 pls*
Jaina ms. dated 1624 A. D. excellent miniature paintings

NAHTA, AGARCHAND	572
'Pandrahvin shati ki Mewar men Chitrit ek Vishistha Prati'
(Hindi)
SP V-2 (Dec 1953) 58-62
Jaina ms. dated V. S. 1480/1423 A. D. made at Delwara (Mewar)

NAHTA, B. L.	573
'Nagaur men Chitrit Apabhramsha Chitra-kala ka Pandava-
Charitra' (Hindi)
SP IX-2 (Dec 1957) 74-81
Pāṇdava-Charitra ms dated V.S. 1468/1411 A. D. made at Nagaur; very
interesting article

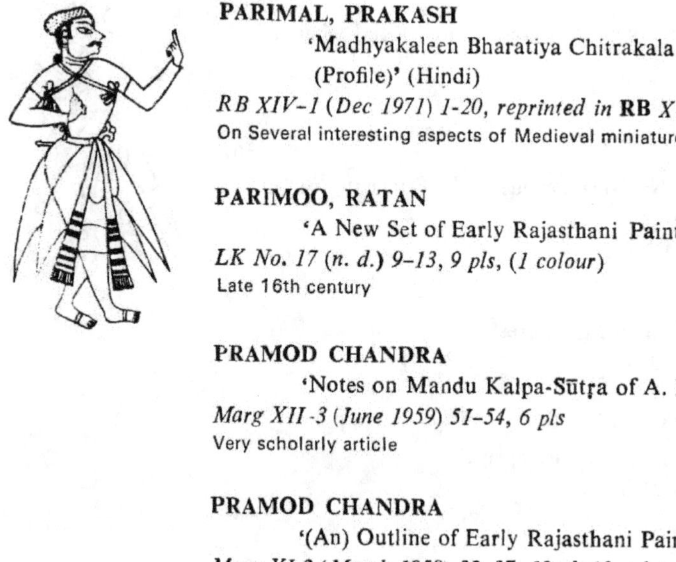

PARIMAL, PRAKASH   574

'Madhyakaleen Bharatiya Chitrakala men ektarfa Mukhakriti (Profile)' (Hindi)

RB XIV-1 (Dec 1971) 1-20, reprinted in **RB** *XV-2 (March 1973) 1-20*

On Several interesting aspects of Medieval miniature painting

PARIMOO, RATAN   575

'A New Set of Early Rajasthani Paintings'

LK No. 17 (n. d.) 9-13, 9 pls, (1 colour)

Late 16th century

PRAMOD CHANDRA   576

'Notes on Mandu Kalpa-Sūtṟa of A. D. 1439'

Marg XII-3 (June 1959) 51-54, 6 pls

Very scholarly article

PRAMOD CHANDRA   577

'(An) Outline of Early Rajasthani Painting'

Marg XI-2 (March 1958) 32-37, 12 pls (2 colour)

PRAMOD CHANDRA   578

'(A) Unique Kālakāchārya Ms. in the Style of the Mandu Kalpa Sūtṟa'

Bulletin of the American Academy Varanasi Vol. I, 1-10 & pls

PUNYAVIJAYA MUNI & SHAH, U. P.   579

'Some Painted Wooden Book-Covers from Western India'

JISOA Special Number (1965-66) 34-44, 14 pls (11 colour)

Of c.12th Century A. D., a very learned article

RAI KRISHNADASA   580

'An Illustrated Avadhi Ms. of Laur-Chandā in the Bharat Kala Bhawan Banaras'

LK 1-2 (April 1955-March 1956) 66-71, 5 pls (1 colour)

Of c. 1540 A. D.

RAI KRISHNADASA   581

'Arambhik Rajasthani Chitro men Ramakatha' (Hindi)

KALA NIDHI Banares 1-4 with pls (1 colour)

On a unique Rāmāyaṇa set of early Rajasthani school in the Kala Bhavan c. 1634 A. D.

SASTRI, N. C.   582

'Jaina-Kala' (Hindi)
JSB XV-2 (Jan 1949) 87-104
Deals usefully also with Jaina Painting

SHAH, U. P.   583

'A Miniature Painting on Bahubali'
PP III-1 (Jan 1975) 15-22

SHAH, U. P.   584

'An Undated Uttaradhayayana Sutra in the Baroda Museum'
BMB XXV (1973-74) 79-86, 10 good pls

SHAH, U. P.   585

'Mahakavi Kalidas-ni Krito-ni Sachitra Prato' (Gujarati)
SB IX-1 (Oct 1971) 111-18, 14 pls
17th century illustrated ms. works of Kalidasa in the Western Indian style of
miniature painting

SHAH, U. P.   586

'(A) Note on Four Paintings of Bhāgavata-Daśama-Skandha'
BMB XXV (1973-74) 87-88, 4 pls

SHAH, U. P.   587

'Shri-Krishna-ni Bal-lila' (Gujarati)
SB X-4 (August 1973) 483-505, 30 pls
Krishna's plays as depicted in sculptures and paintings e.g. in Balagopalastuti of
Kankroli etc

SHAH, U. P.   588

'Solama Saikani Gujarati Chitra-Shaili' (Gujarati)
SB VII-1 (Nov 1969) 57-63, 14 excellent pls
Gujarati style of painting in the 16th century

SHAH, U. P.   589

'Two New Documents of Painting from Muni Punyavijayaji's
Collection'
Chhavi (1971) 151-56 with pls
Of Western Indian School of Painting, 16th century A. D.

SINGH, CHANDRAMANI   590
'An Illustrated Ms. from Malavadesa dated V. S. 1820'
JJ I. 3-4 (July-Oct 1974) 95-98

SKELTON, ROBERT   591
(The) Ni'mat-Nāmah : A Landmark in Malwa Painting'
Marg XII-3 (June 1959) 44-50, 14 pls (2 colour)
Illustrated at Mandu 1500-1510; a learned enumeration

5

MINIATURE PAINTING :
(C) Chinese, Persian & Turkish Painting
(A Source of Mughal Miniature Art)

BOOKS

ANAND, M. R.; TITLEY, NORAH; GRAY, BASIL; & ROBINSON, B. W. 592
    'Persian Painting : 15th Century'
(Marg Bombay 1977) with colour and monotone pls

ARBERRY, A. J.; MINOVI, M. & BLOCHET, E. 593
    '(The) Chester Beatty Library, A Catalogue of the Persian Mss.
      and Miniatures' 2 vols
(Dublin 1959)

ARNOLD, T. W. 594
    'Bihzād and his Paintings in the Zafar-Nāmah Ms.'
(London 1930) pp. 24, 15 pls

ARNOLD, T. W. 595
    'Painting in Islam : A Study of the Place of Pictorial Art in
      Muslim Culture'
(Oxford. London 1928; Dover New York 1965) xviii+159, 65 pls
On Philosophy origin and development of Muslim Painting

ARNOLD, T. W. & GROHMANN, A. 596
    '(The) Islamic Book'
(London 1929)
Valuable references to Mughal miniature paintings

ASHTON, L. & GRAY, B. 597
'Chinese Art'
(*London 1951*)

ASLANAPA, O. 598
1. 'Turkish Arts' (*Istambul 1961*)
2. 'Turkish Art & Architecture' (*London 1971*)

BACHHOFER, L. 599
'(A) Short History of Chinese Art'
(*New York 1946*)

BARRETT, DOUGLAS; TITLEY, NORAH & ANAND, M. R. 600
'Persian Painting of the 14th Century'
(*Marg Bombay 1977*)
Gives a learned historical background since the Ilkhans; also analyses Chinese
and other influences

BINNEY, E. 601
'Islamic Art from the collection of Edwin Binney 3rd'
(*Washington, D. C. 1966*)
Reviewed by Karl J. Khandalavala in the LK No. 15 (1972) 61-62

BINYON, LAURENCE 602
'(The) Flight of the Dragon : An Essay'
(*London 1911*)

BINYON, LAURENCE 603
'Painting in the Far East'
(*Dover, New York 1959*)
Though essentially he deals with Japanese and Chinese paintings, he also
discusses Chinese influence on Persian Painting; discusses Bihzad and his art
and other aspects

BINYON, LAURENCE 604
'(The) Spirit of Man in Asian Art'
(*London 1935*)

BINYON, LAURENCE; WILKINSON J. V. S. & GRAY, B. 605
'Persian Miniature Painting'
(including a Critical and Descriptive Catalogue of the
Miniatures exhibited at Burlington House, Jan-March 1931)
(*London 1933*)

BINYON, LAURENCE & WILKINSON, J. V. S.   606
'(The) Shāh-Nāmah of Firdausi'
(*London 1931*)

BLOCHET, E.   607
'Musalman Painting'
(12th–13th century A. D.)
(tr. by C. M. Binyon)
(*London 1929*)

BURLING, F.   608
'Chinese Art'
(*London 1954*)

CAHILL, J. B.   609
'Chinese Painting'
(*New York 1960*)

CHAGHTAI, M. A.   610
'A Treatise on Calligraphists and Miniaturists by Dost
Muhammad the Librarian of Bahram Mirza (d. 1550 A. D.)'
(Persian)
(*Lahore 1936*)
A grand treatise on 16th century Persian Painting

CLARK, SIR K.   611
'Landscape into Art'
(*London 1949*)

COHN, W.   612
'Chinese Art'
(*London 1930*)

COHN, W.   613
'Chinese Painting'
(*London 1948*)

DE SILVA, ANIL   614
'Chinese Landscape Painting'
(*London 1967*)

DIMAND, M. S.   **615**
  ‘(A) Handbook of Mohammedan Decorative Art’
(*New York 1930*)
Pp. 17-65 deal with Persian Painting

ETTINGHAUSEN, R.   **616**
  ‘Bihzād’
The Encyclopaedia of Islam, Vol. I. (London 1960) 1211-14
On the life and work of the famous 15th century Persian painter; the article
also includes a detailed bibliography on Bihzad and Persian Painting

ETTINGHAUSEN, R.   **617**
  ‘Turkish Miniatures from the 13th to 18th century’
(*Milano Fontana, Unesco Art Books, 1965*)

FEDDERSEN, MARTIN   **618**
  ‘Chinese Decorative Art’
(*London 1961*)

FENOLLOSA, ERNEST F.   **619**
  ‘Epochs of Chinese and Japanese Art’
  Vol. I
(*Dover New York 1963*)

GRAY, B.   **620**
  ‘Masterpieces of Persian Miniature Painting’
(*New York 1940*)

GRAY, B.   **621**
  ‘Persian Painting’
(*London 1961*) *with pls*

GRAY, B.   **622**
  ‘Persian Painting from Miniatures of the 13th-16th centuries’
(*London 1948*)

GRAY, B.; DIGBY, SIMON; TITLEY, NORAH & Others   **623**
  ‘Arts of the Book’
in the ‘**Arts of Islam**’ *The Arts Council of Great Britain (London 1976)*
pp. 309-72, with excellent pls

GRAY, BASIL & GODARD, ANDRE   624
    'Iran'
    (Persian Miniatures-Imperial Library)
(*Unesco World Art Series, Paris 1957*)
Deals wlth Miniature and Mural Painting; discusses Bihzad and the Chinese
influence

GRUBE, E. J.   625
    '(The) Classical Style in Islamic Painting : The Early School
    of Herat and its Impact on Islamic Painting of the Later
    15th-16th-17th Centuries'
(*New York 1968*)

GRUBE, E. J.   626
    'Islamic Paintings from the 11th to the 18th Century'
    (The Collection of Hans P. Kraus)
(*New York 1971*)

GRUBE, E. J.   627
    'Muslim Miniature Paintings from the 13th to 19th Century
    from Collections in the United States & Canada'
(*Venice 1962*)

GRUBE, E. J.   628
    '(The World of Islam'
(*Landmarks of the World's Art Series, Paul Hamlyn, London 1966*)
Deals with mural and miniature paintings of Muslim countries with exquisite
illustrations

GUEST, G. D.   629
    'Shiraz Painting in the Sixteenth Century'
 Washington 1949)

HUART, C.   630
    'Les Calligraphes et les Miniaturistes de l' Orient Musulman'
    (French)
(*Paris 1908*)
A grand treatise on Calligraphy and Miniature Painting

LEE, S. E.   631
    'Chinese Landscape Painting'
(*Cleveland 1954*)

LEE, S. E.   632
    '(A) History of Far Eastern Art'
(*London 1964*)

LIN YUTANG   633
    '(The) Chinese Theory of Art'
(*London 1967*)
Deals authoritatively with various limbs of Painting, e. g. Tchi or Rhythmic Vitality

MARTIN, F. R.   634
    '(The) Miniature Painting & Painters of Persia, India and
    Turkey from 8th to 18th century'
    2 vols
(*London 1912*)

MEREDITH–OWENS, G. M.   635
    'Persian Illustrated Mss.'
(*British Museum Publication, London 1973*)
Miniature Painting of Persia

MEREDITH–OWENS, G. M.   636
    'Turkish Miniatures'
(*London 1963*)

MINORSKY, V. & MINORSKY, T.   637
    'Calligraphers and Painters—A Treatise by Qazi Ahmed son
    of Mir Munshi'
(*Washington, 1959*)

MINORSKY, V. & WILKINSON, J. V. S.   638
    '(A) Catalogue of Turkish Manuscripts and Miniatures'
    (The Chester Beatty Library)
(*Dublin 1958*)

PAPADOPOULO, ALEXANDRE   639
    'Islam & Muslim Art'
    (tr. from French by Robert Erich Wolf)
(*Thames & Hudson London 1980*) *1118 pls* (*174 colour*)
Deals elaborately with Architecture, Mural and Miniature Painting

PINDER-WILSON, R. H.   640

     'Persian Painting of the 15th century'
(*London 1958*)

POPE, A. U.   641

     '(An) Introduction to Persian Art'
(*London 1930*)
Its pp. 99-117 deal with the Persian Art of the book (Miniature Painting)
(with pls)

POPE, A. U.   642

     'Survey of Persian Art'
(*London 1939*)
Its Vol. III pp.1809 onwards on the Philosophy, Aesthetics, origins and other
aspects of Persian Painting; a very scholarly enumeration of the Art History

PRIEST, A.   643

     'Aspects of Chinese Painting'
(*New York 1954*)

RICE, D. T.   644

     'Islamic Art'
(*London 1965*)
Also deals with miniature painting usefully

RICE, D. T.   645

     'Islamic Painting : A Survey'
(*Edinburgh 1971*)

ROBINSON, B. W.   646

     'Persian Paintings'
(*Victoria & Albert Museum London 1965*)
A Catalogue of 36 paintings

ROBINSON, B. W. & GRAY, B.   647

     '(The) Persian Art of the Book'
(*Rome 1972*)
On Miniature Painting of Persia, with pls

**ROBINSON, B. W.; GRUBE, E. J.; MEREDITH-OWENS, G. M. &
SKELTON, R. W.**   648

'Islamic Painting and the Arts of the Book'
(*Faber & Faber London 1976*)
Its Part-III 'Persian & Pre-Mughal Indian Painting' by B. W. Robinson, catalogue
of 424 miniatures, with many colour pls; Part-V 'Indian Painting of the Mughal
Period' by R. W. Skelton, catalogue of 105 miniatures with colour pls

ROWLEY, G.   649

'Principles of Chinese Painting'
(*Princeton 1947*)

SICKMAN, L. & SOPER, A. C.   650

'(The) Art and Architecture of China'
(*Pelican History of Art, London 1956*)

SILVA, ANIL DE   651

'Chinese Landscape Painting'
(*London 1967*)

SIREN, O.   652

'(The) Chinese on the Art of Painting'
(*Peking 1936*)
On the Theory of Chinese Painting; a very valuable work

SIREN, O.   653

'History of Early Chinese Art'
4 vols
(*London 1929-30*)

SIREN, O.   654

'(A) History of Early Chinese Painting'
2 vols
(*London 1933*)

SOURDEL-THOMINE, J.   655

'Fann' (Art)
The Encyclopaedia of Islam, *II* (*London 1965*) 775-78
A general study of the concept of Art in Islam with a useful bibliography

SPEISER, WERNER   **656**

'China' (Spirit & Society)
(*Art of the World Series, tr. by George Lawrence, London 1960*)
Also a detailed enumeration of Chinese Painting

SULLIVAN, MICHAEL   **657**

'Chinese & Japanese Art'
(*The Book of Art Series, Vol. 9 Grolier, London 1965*)
Also deals with Painting

SULLIVAN, MICHAEL   **658**

'(An) Introduction to Chinese Art'
(*London 1961*)

SULLIVAN, MICHAEL   **659**

'On the Origin of Landscape Representation in Chinese Art'
(*Archives of the Chinese Art Society of America, Vol. VII,
New York 1953*)

WALEY, A.   **660**

'(An) Introduction to the Study of Chinese Painting'
(*London 1923*)

WHITE, W. C.   **661**

'Chinese Temple Frescoes'
(*Toronto 1940*)

WILLETTS, W.   **662**

'Chinese Art'
2 vols
(*Harmondsworth 1958*)

—   **663**

'XVI Century Miniatures Illustrating Manuscript Copies
of the Works of Jami from the U. S. S. R. Collections'
(*Moscow n. d*) *pp, 92, 55 colour pls of superb quality, Russian with
English trans.*

ARTICLES

AGA-OGLU, MEHMET   **664**
'(The) Landscape Miniatures of An Anthology
Manuscript of the year A. D. 1398'
Ars Islamica III (1936) 77-98, 9 pls

AMJAD ALI, S.   **665**
'Muslim Painting'
Pakistan Quarterly, II-4 (1952) 8-13, 63-64, 10 illus. (2 colour)

ANAND, M. R.   **666**
'(The) Emergence of Style in 14th Century Persian Painting'
Marg XXX-1 (Dec. 1976) 5-9

ANAND, M. R.   **667**
'(The) Sources of Creative Art in Persia in the Early
Medieval Centuries'
Marg XXX-1 (Dec 1976) 11-37, 20 pls
Also deals with the beginnings of Persian Painting

ANAND, M. R.   **668**
'(The) Turkish Heritage in Painting' &
'Portfolio'
Marg XXVI-4 (Sept 1973) 2-8 & pls

ANIS FAROOQI   **669**
'Persian Painting under the Safavids'
II XXVI-4 (Dec 1973) 17-27, 3 pls
Gives valuable information on Bihzad; a very interesting and useful article

BARRETT, DOUGLAS   **670**
'Unveiling "The Face of Persian Painting" '
Marg XXX-1 (Dec 1976) 3-4
Being foreword to this special Number on Persian Painting

BOGDANOR, L.   **671**
'A Persian Miniature of the XVI Century'
IsC V-2 (April 1931)

BUCHTHAL, HUGO   672
'Indian Fables in Islamic Art'
Journal of the Royal Asiatic Society London 1941, 317-24
On the depiction of Panchtantra stories in Miniature Painting

CAGMAN, F.   673
'Ottomon Turkish Miniatures'
Marg XXVI-4 (Sept 1973) 29-54, 37 excellent pls
A very useful survey

CRESWELL, K. A. C.   674
'(The) Lawfulness of Painting in Early Islam'
Ars Islamica XI-XII (1946) 159-66; reprinted in the
IsC XXIV (1950) 218-30

CRESWELL, K. A. C.   675
'(The) Lawfulness of Painting in Islam'
IsC XXIV (1950) 218-30

CRESWELL, K. A. C.   676
'Note on the Attitude of Islam Towards Painting'
Bulletin of the Faculty of Arts, Fouad I University VII (1944) 16-17
A reply to Zaki's article on the same subject published in the same issue
pp. 1-15

DIMAND, M. S.   677
'Islamic Miniature Painting and Book Illumination'
Bulletin of Metropolitan Museum of Art XXVIII (1933)
166-71, with pls

DIMAND, M S.   678
'Oriental Miniatures'
Bulletin of the Metropolitan Museum of Art XX (1925)
124-28, 6 ills.
Deals with 14 Persian Miniatures

FISCHER, KLAUS   679
'Haft-Paikar Illustrations in a Nizami Ms.'
II VIII-2 (June 1955) 1-7, 3 pls & 6 figs
Interesting information about bulbous dome and its depiction in painting

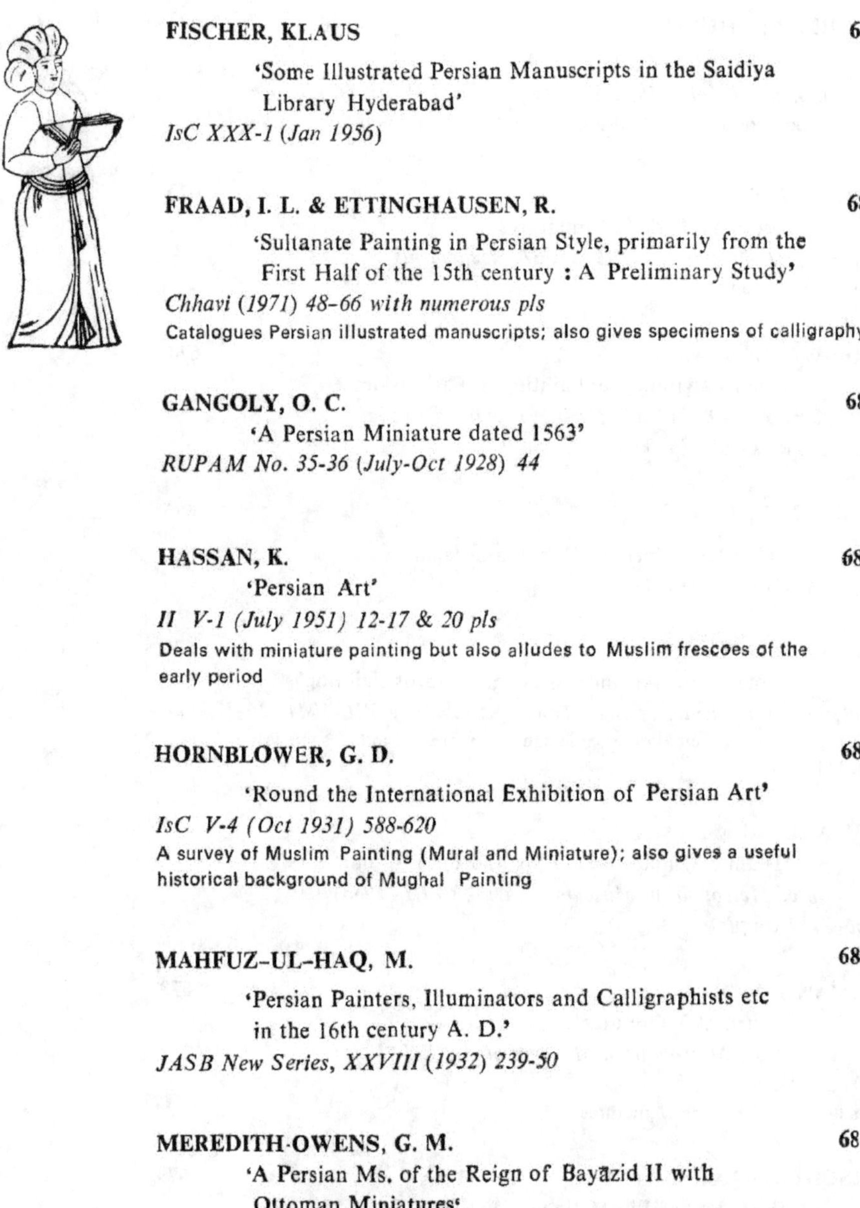

FISCHER, KLAUS   680

'Some Illustrated Persian Manuscripts in the Saidiya
Library Hyderabad'
IsC XXX-1 (Jan 1956)

FRAAD, I. L. & ETTINGHAUSEN, R.   681

'Sultanate Painting in Persian Style, primarily from the
First Half of the 15th century : A Preliminary Study'
Chhavi (1971) 48-66 with numerous pls
Catalogues Persian illustrated manuscripts; also gives specimens of calligraphy

GANGOLY, O. C.   682

'A Persian Miniature dated 1563'
RUPAM No. 35-36 (July-Oct 1928) 44

HASSAN, K.   683

'Persian Art'
II V-1 (July 1951) 12-17 & 20 pls
Deals with miniature painting but also alludes to Muslim frescoes of the
early period

HORNBLOWER, G. D.   684

'Round the International Exhibition of Persian Art'
IsC V-4 (Oct 1931) 588-620
A survey of Muslim Painting (Mural and Miniature); also gives a useful
historical background of Mughal Painting

MAHFUZ-UL-HAQ, M.   685

'Persian Painters, Illuminators and Calligraphists etc
in the 16th century A. D.'
JASB New Series, XXVIII (1932) 239-50

MEREDITH-OWENS, G. M.   686

'A Persian Ms. of the Reign of Bayāzid II with
Ottoman Miniatures'
BPOW No. 10 (1967) 27-31, 7 pls ·
Of the latter half of the 16th century A. D.

NIZAMUDDIN, M.   687
    'A Unique Illustrated Ms. of Sā'dī's Gulistān'
Dr G. Yazdani Commemoration Vol. Hyderabad (1966) pp. 121-26, 4 pls
Persian Miniature painting 1570 A. D.

ROBINSON, B. W.   688
    '(The) Durham Gulistan : An Unpublished Timurid
      Manuscript'
Oriental Art Oxford XXII-1 (1976) 52-59 & pls
15th century Persian paintings

SUHRAWARDY, SHAHID   689
    'Introduction to the Study of Indo–Persian Painting'
Marg XI-3 (June 1958)   21-29, 19 pls
Historical background of Mughal painting

TITLEY, NORAH   690
    ·Development of 14th-15th Century Painting in Khorasan
      Iran & Turkey'
Marg XXVI-4 (Sept 1973) 17-28 & 28 excellent pls

TITLEY, NORAH   691
    'Persian Painting of the 14th, 15th and 16th centuries and its
      influence on Indian Painting'
Marg XXVIII-3 (June 1975) 13-18, 10 pls (3 Colour)

TITLEY, NORAH   692
    'Fourteenth Century Persian Painting : A Survey'
Marg XXX-1 (Dec 1976) 38-60, 25 excellent pls
A very informative survey

WIENER, ERNST COHN   693
    'On the Origin of the Persian Carpet Pattern'
IsC XI-4 (Oct 1937)

ZAKI, M. H.   694
    '(The) Attitude of Islam Towards Figurative Painting'
The Islamic Review Woking. XLIV No. 7 (1956) 24-29, 1 illus.

ZAKI, M. H. 695

'(The) Attitude of Islam Towards Painting'
Bulletin of the Faculty of Arts, Fouad I University, Vol. VIII (1944) 1–15
His views are replied by Creswell in the same issue pp. 16-17

ZAKI, M. H. 696

'(The) Lawfulness of Painting in Islam'
The Islamic Review Woking, XLI (1953) No. 6, p. 29

MINIATURE PAINTING
(D) Mughal
(Durbari & Popular)

BOOKS

AB'UL FAZL   697

    'Āin-i- Akbarī'
Vol. I English tr. by H. Blochmann (Calcutta 1871, reprinted Delhi 1965)
Ain-34 (pp. 102-15 entitled : **'Art of Writing and Painting'** deals with painting and painters of the time of Akbar

ALVI, M. A. & RAHMAN. A.   698

    'Jahangir, the Naturalist'
(New Delhi 1968)
Valuable references to Jahangir's miniatures

ANIS FAROOQI   699

    'Art of India and Persia'
(New Delhi 1979) pp. 104 & pls
Mughal painting and its sources chiefly Persian

BINNEY, EDWIN   700

    'Indian Miniatures from the Collection of Edwin Binney
    3rd : The Mughal and Deccani School with some related
    Sultanate Material'
(Portland Art Museum Portland Oregon 1973)

BINYON, L. & ARNOLD, T. 701

'(The) Court Painters of the Grand Moghuls'
(*Oxford, 1921*)

BROWN, PERCY 702

'Indian Painting under the Mughals' (1550-1750)
(*Oxford 1924, reprinted New Delhi 1981) pp. 204, 72 pls*

CLARKE, C. STANLEY 703

'Indian Drawings: Thirty Mogul Paintings of the School of
Jahangir in the Wantage Bequest'
(*London 1922*) Reprinted Cosmo New Delhi, 1983, See its review in IJ - II

CLARKE, C. STANLEY 704

'Indian Drawings : Twelve Mogul Paintings of the
School of Humayun, Illustrating the Romance of
Amir Hamza'
(*London 1921*)

COOMARASWAMY, A. K. 705

'Catalogue of the Indian Collections in the Museums of
Fine Arts : Part VI : Moghul Paintings'
(*Cambridge, Mass 1930*)

CRESWELL, K. A. C. 706

'A Bibliography of Architecture, Arts and Crafts of Islam,
to 1st January 1960'
(*The American University at Cairo Press 1961*)
Its pp. 1047 to 1073 contain useful entries on Mughal Painting in English, French
and German; there are no entries from Hindi or other vernacular journals of India
which also contain a wealth of data; most of the Western journals listed in it are
not normally available to Indian scholar; it is upto 1959 and much valuable
material on the subject has been published in the meantime, the entries have
thus to be updated

DAS, A K. 707

'Mughal Painting during the Time of Jahangir'
(*The Asiatic Society Calcutta 1978) xxiii+279
and 81 pls*

DIHLAVI, GHULAM MUHAMMAD   708
  'Tazkirā-i-Khushnavīsān' (Persian)
(Ed. by M. Hidayat Husain Bib. Ind. Calcutta 1910)
A valuable account of Mughal calligraphers and painters

ETTINGHAUSEN, R.   709
  'Paintings of Sultans and Emperors of India in American
      Collection'
(Lalit Kala Akademi New Delhi 1961)
Reviewed in the **LK** No. 9 (April 1961) 68-69

HAJEK, LUBOR   710
  'Indian Miniatures of the Moghul School'
(London 1960)

HENDLEY, T. H.   711
  '(The) Razm-Nāmah Manuscript'
Memorials of the Jeypore Exhibition London 1883, Vol. 4

JAHANGIR, NURUDDIN BADSHAH   712
  'Tuzuk-i-Jahangiri'
*English tr. by A. Rogers & H. Beveridge, 2 vols : 'Memoirs of
Jahangir' (London 1909-14 reprinted in one volume New Delhi 1968)*
Autobiography of the Mughal Emperor Jahangir the greatest of the Mughal
connoisseurs of Miniature Painting; this work is a valuable source of Mughal
Painting of his period

KUHNEL, ERNST & GOETZ, HERMANN   713
  'Indian Book Painting'
(London 1926)
On the famous Album of Mughal miniatures viz. Jahangir's **Muraqqa-i-
Gulshan'**; a very useful work

LAWRENCE, GEORGE   714
  'Indian Art - Mughal Miniatures'
(London)

MARTIN, F. R.   715
  '(The) Miniature Painting and Painters of Persia India
      and Turkey'
(Quaritch London 1912)

MOTICHANDRA 716
'Technique of Mughal Painting'
(*Lucknow 1949*)

PINDER–WILSON, R. (ed.) 717
'Paintings from Islamic Lands'
(*Bruno Cassirer Oxford 1969*)
Reviewed by Khandalavala in the **LK** No. 15 (1972) 60-61

PRAMOD CHANDRA 718
'Tuti–Nama' 2 vols
(*Cleveland Museum 1976*)
Excellent commentary on the Early Mughal miniatures of the Akbari period,
Fascimile Volume-II with superb reproductions of those paintings

RAI KRISHNADAS 719
'Mughal Miniatures'
(Introduction by Humayun Kabir)
(*Lalit Kala Academy New Delhi 1955*)
Reviewed in the **LK** 1-2 (April 1955-March 1956) 148-52 with 1 colour pl

RAY, NIHARRANJAN 720
'Mughal Court Painting : A Study in Social and Formal
Analysis'
(*Indian Museum Calcutta 1975*) *pp. 226, 33 pls in colour*

SOLOMON, W. E. G. 721
'Essays on Mughal Art'
(*Bombay 1932, IBH Reprint Varanasi 1972*) *pp. 96, 18 pls*
Interesting articles on Mughal Painting

TYULAYEV, S. 722
'Miniatures of Babur-Namah'
(*Moscow 1960*)

VERMA, S. P. 723
'Art and Material Culture in the Paintings of Akbar's
Court'
(*Vikas New Delhi 1978*) *pp. 150, 78 pls*
Reviewed **IsC** LIV-2 (April 1980) 130-32

WELCH, STUART CARY   724
>'(The) Art of Mughal India'
>(Painting and Precious Objects)

(New York 1963)

WELLESZ, EMMY   725
>'Akbar's Religious Thought as reflected in Mogul
>Painting'

(London 1952)

WILKINSON, J. V. S.   726
>'Mughal Painting' (with Introduction and Notes)

(London 1968)
Survey of Mughal Painting from Hamzā Nāmah to Shah Jehan; also deals with various influences : Persian and European

—   727
>'Indian Archaeology : A Review'

1953-54 to 1977-78 (Archaeological Survey of India New Delhi)
Each volume has a section on museums which gives valuable references to palm-leaf and paper illustrated manuscripts, miniatures and porrtaits from 11th to 19th century of various schools, with illustrations

—   728
>'Miniatures of Bābur Nāmah'

(Moscow 1960)
With excellent colour plates and a brief Introduction in English

ARTICLES

ANAND KRISHNA   729
>'A Living Hereditary Artist of the Mughal School'

LK 1–2 (April 1955-March 1956) 77–78, 4 pls
On Sharda Prasad son of Ustad Ram Prasad living at Banares

ANAND KRISHNA   730
>'(A) Reassessment of the Tuti-Nama illustrations in
>the Cleveland Museum of Art (and related problems
>on Earliest Mughal Paintings and Painters)'

AA XXXV–3 (1973) 241–68, 13 pls

ANAND KRISHNA 731
'(A) Study of the Akbari Artist : Farrukh Chela'
Chhavi (1971) 353-73, with numerous beautiful pls
A very learned and useful article

ANAND, M. R. 732
'(The) Background of Early Mughal Painting'
Marg XI-3 (June 1958) 30-33, 19 pls

ANAND, M. R. 733
'Indian Painting' (at the Victoria & Albert Museum)
Marg XXIX-4 (Sept 1976) 31-56, 20 pls (including colour)
Paintings from the Hamzā-Nāmah and Akbar-Nāmah also

ANAND, M. R. 734
'Painting–Jehangir the Epicurean'
Marg XI-4 (Sept 1958) 26-32, 11 pls (2 colour)

ANAND, M. R. 735
'Portraits'
'Birds & Animals'
Marg XI-4 (Sept 1958) 42-47, 17 pls
Mostly of Jehangir's reign; birds by Ustād Mansūr

ANIS FAROOQI 736
'(A) Critical Study of Indo-Persian Style of Painting'
IsC XLVIII-4 (Oct 1974) 247-52

ANIS FAROOQI 737
'(The) Establishment of Akbar's Atelier'
IB XI-1 (March 1974) 33-41
Its formation, composition and working

ANIS FAROOQI 738
'Painters of Akbar's Court'
IsC XLVIII-2 (April 1974) 119-26
Names all the artists of his atelier; a very useful catalogue

ANIS FAROOQI 739
'Pigments and Materials used in Indian and Persian
            Miniatures'
IsC LI-1 (Jan 1977) 11-19

ANIS FAROOQI   740
  'Reassessment on the Commencement of the Dastan-i-Amir
  Hamzah'
Roop-Lekha XLII 1-2 (no date) 35-37
The author argues that the work began by order of Akbar c. 1558 and
finished in 1573 A. D.

ARNOLD, T. W.   741
  'An Indian Picture of Muhammad and His Companions'
Burlington Magazine XXXIV (1919) 249-53, 1 pl
On the lawfulness of figurative art and painting in Islam

ASHRAF, M.   742
  '(The) Decline' (Of Mughal Painting)
Marg XI-4 (Sept 1958) 55-57, 3 pls
Post-Shahjehanian era

BEACH, M. C.   743
  'A European Source for Early Mughal Painting'
Oriental Art Oxford XXII-2 (1976) 180-88, 13 pls
Paintings of Akbar's period

BINNEY, E. (3rd)   744
  'Later Mughal Painting'
In **'Aspects of Indian Art'** *(ed. by P. Pal)*
(Brill, Leiden 1972) 118-23, 10 pls
Mainly of the 18th century

BLUNT, W.   745
  '(The) Mughal Painters of Natural History'
The Burlington Magazine London XC (1948) 49-50
His hypothesis is more imaginary than documented

BOGDANOR, L.   746
  'Indo-Persian and Modern Indian Paintings'
IsC V-1 (Jan 1931)

BUKHARI, Y. K.   747
  'A Rare Manuscript on Calligraphy'
IsC XXXVII-2 (April 1963) 92-99 5 pls
Originally composed and dedicated to Alamgir (Aurangzib) in 1690 A. D.

CHAGHTAI, M. A. 748
'Emperor Jahangir's Interviews with Gosain Jadrup
and His Portraits'
IsC XXXVI-2 (April 1962) 119-28, 2 pls
Very learned and useful enumeration.

CHAGHTAI, M. A. 749
'(A) Few Hindu Miniature-Painters of the 18th and 19th
century'
IsC VIII-3 (July 1934) 397-98

CHAGHTAI, M. A. 750
'(The) Illustrated Edition of the Razm Namah at
Akbar's Court'
*Bulletin of the Deccan College Research Institute Poona
V (1943-44) 281-329*

CHAGHTAI, M. A. 751
'Mir Sayyid Ali Tabrezi'
Pakistan Quarterly IV-4 (1954) 24-25, 1 fig.
One of the two earliest Mughal Painters brought to India from Persia by
Humayun.

CODRINGTON, K. de B. 752
'(The) Animals in Art : Indian'
Geographical Magazine CIV (1944) 208-16

COHN-WIENER, ERNEST 753
'Miniatures of Razm Namah from Akbar's Time'
IAL XII (1938) 90-92
Gives only a brief appraisal.

COOMARASWAMY, A. K. 754
'Khwajah Khadir and the Fountain of Life, in the
Tradition of Persian and Mughal Art'
Ars Islamica Michigan I-2 (1934) 173-82, 2 pls
Related to Miniature Painting.

COOMARASWAMY, A. K. 755
'Notes on Indian Paintings'
*AA II-1 (1927) 5-11, 5 pls; its Part-II in II-2 pp.132-37, 5 pls;
Part-III in II-3, 202-12, 10 pls and Part IV in II-4, 283-94, 5 pls*
Under the title 'A Contribution to Mughal Iconography' in first two parts he
discusses a few Mughal portraits in the third he deals with Miniature Painting
and in the fourth he deals with Bishndas and other Mughal artists.

COOMARASWAMY, A. K.   756
'Originality in Mughal Painting'
Journal of Royal Asiatic Society London 1910, 874-81

DAS, A. K.   757
'Bishndas'
CHHAVI (1971) 183-91 with several excellent pls
On Jehangir's famous miniature painter

DAS, A. K.   758
'European Elements in Early Mughal Painting with Special
Reference to the Collections of the Victoria Memorial and
the Indian Museum Calcutta'
*Bulletin of the School of Oriental & African Studies London
XXVIII-3 (1975) 24-28*

DAS, A. K.   759
'Mughal Royal Hunt in Miniature Painting'
IMB II-1 (Jan 1967) 19-23

DAS, A. K.   760
'Notes on a Portrait of Prince Khurram in the Victoria
Memorial'
Bulletin of the Victoria Memorial Calcutta, III-IV (1969-70) 6-7

DAS, A. K.   761
'Ustad Mansur'
LK 17 (n.d.) pp.32-39, 5 pls
On the famous painter of Jehangir Ustad Mansur Naqqash; also see his **'Some
More Mansur Drawings' LK No. 18, 26-31, 4 pls**; along with a learned enume-
ration, he also lists Mansur's paintings; gives full information and references on
the subject.

DIMAND, M. S.   762
'(An) Exhibition of Islamic and Indian Painting'
*Bulletin of the Metropolitan Museum of Art New York
XIV (1955) 85-102*

DIMAND, M. S.   763
'Mughal Painting under Akbar the Great'
Bulletin of the Metropolitan Museum of Art New York XII (1953)

DIMAND, M. S.   764
    'Several Illustrations from the Dāstān-i-Amīr Hamzā
    in American Collections'
AA XI. 1-2 (1948) 5-13. 5 pls
Very useful study with an adequate historical background

FABRI, C. L.   765
    'Ballet Costume in Akbar's Time'
Marg VII-1 (Dec 1953) 17-22, 2 pls and 4 figs
Study is based on miniature paintings of Akbar

GANGOLY, A. N.   766
    'A Moghul Miniature from the Lahore Museum'
RUPAM Nos. 38-39 (April-July 1929) 78-84
Also refers to other Mughal paintings showing Harem Life

GANGOLY, O. C.   767
    'An Illustrated Ms. of Anvār-i-Suhailī : A New Version'
RUPAM Nos. 42-44 (April-Oct 1930) 11-14

GOETZ, H.   768
    'An Early Mughal Portrait of Sultān 'Abdullah Qutbshāh of
    Golconda (1626-72)'
BMB III–1 (1945-46) 31–33

GOETZ, H.   769
    'An Illustration from the Hamzā-Nāmah, the Earliest
    Mughal Ms.'
BMB II-1 (1944-45) 31-34 & pl

GOETZ, H.   770
    '(The) Early Muraqqas of the Mughal Emperor Jahangir'
Marg XI-4 (Sept 1958) 33-41, 4 pls
Miniature paintings with beautiful ornamented Hāshiyahs (margins)

GOETZ, H.   771
    'Early Oudh School of Mughal Painting'
BMB IX (1952-53) 9-24
A very useful article

GOETZ, H.   772
    'Hindu Element in Indo-Muslim Art'
RAA (Wiesbaden 1978) 31-38
Attempts to analyse influences on Mughal Painting

GOETZ, H.   773
> 'Life and Art in the Mughal Period : The Mental Background
> of Mughal Painting and its Reflection in Art'

Journal of the University of Bombay V-4 (1937) 55-67
An interesting article

GOETZ, H.   774
> 'Masterpieces of Mogul Painting'
> (The Album of Emperor Jehangir)

Marg VI–2 (March 1953) 39-44, 10 pls
Best specimens of the Art of Hāshiyas (Margins)

GOETZ, H.   775
> '(The) Problem of the Origin of two Medieval Indo-Persian
> Miniatures'

IsC XXIX-3 (July 1955) 179–83 and pls

GOETZ, H.   776
> 'Vestiges of Muslim Painting under the Sultans of Gujarat
> (15th-16th century A. D.)'

Journal of the Gujarat Research Society Bombay III (1954) 212-20,
11 illustrations

GOSWAMY, B. N. & DALLAPICCOLA, A. L.   777
> '(A) Tuti-Nama from Gujarat, A Dated and Illustrated
> Manuscript in the Von Portheim-Stiftung Heidelberg'

AA XXXVIII-4 (1976) 287-296, 12 pls
Written at Baroda in 1054/1644-45 late style with Persian and local influences.
Jahangiri hāshiyahs also appear

GRAY, BASIL   778
> 'A Mughal Drawing'

British Museum Quarterly LIII (1938-39) 72-73

GRAY, BASIL   779
> '(The) Development of Painting in India in the 16th century'

Marg VI-3 (June 1953) 19-24, 6 pls
A very learned survey

GRAY, BASIL   780
> 'Intermingling of Mogul and Rajput Art'

Marg VI-2 (March 1953) 36-38, 2 pls

HIDAYAT, A. 781

'Shah Jehan'
Marg XI-4 (Sept 1959) 48-49, 12 pls
Miniature Painting under Shah Jehan.

JAYASWAL, P. K. 782

'(The) So-called Bazar Mughal School Paintings'
LK No. 15 (1972) 56
On the classification of Mughal Miniature Painting under three heads : Imperial,
Popular and Bazar; the author elaborates the criteria of distinction between the
Popular and the Bazar; a very interesting pointer.

KALYAN KRISHNA 783

'Problems of a Portrait of Jahangir in the Musee Guimet,
Paris'
CHHAVI (1971) 392-94 with pls

KHANDALAVALA, KARL J. 784

'A Mughal Miniature of Prince Khurram'
BMB X-XI (1953-55) 1-5

KHANDALAVALA, KARL J. 785

'An Akbar Period Mughal Miniature Illustration of
Gita-Govinda'
Roop-Lekha II-3 (1942) 49-55 and pls

KHANDALAVALA, KARL J. 786

'Eighteenth Century Mughal Painting'
(Some Characteristics and Some Misconceptions)
Marg XI-4 (Sept 1959) 58-61, 4 pls

KHANDALAVALA, KARL J. 787

'Five Miniatures : In the Collection of Sir Cowasji Jehangir
Bombay'
Marg V-2 (March 1952) 24-32, 5 pls
2 Deccani (17th century), 2 Mughal (17th) and 1 Kishangarh (mid-18th century)

KHANDALAVALA, KARL J. 788

'Some Problems of Mughal Painting'
LK No. 11 (April 1962) 9-13, 5 figs 1 colour pl
A very interesting article dealing with some basic problems.

KHANDALAVALA, KARL J. & JAGDISH MITTAL   789
    'An Early Akbari Illustrated Ms. of Tilasm and Zodiac'
LK No. 14 (1969) 9–20, 36 pls
On an Akbari ms. containing amils (Talismans) done c. 1567-70;
an extremely informative and useful paper

LEE, SHERMAN & PRAMODCHANDRA   790
    'A Newly Discovered Tuti-Namah and the Continuity of the
    Indian Tradition of Ms. Painting'
The Burlington Magazine London Vol. CV No. 729 (1963)

LOEWENSTEIN, FELIX   791
    'Saint Magdalene-or Bibi Rabia Basri in Mogul Painting'
IsC XIII-4 (Oct 1939) 466–69, 3 pls

LOKHANDWALA, M. F.   792
    'Jahangir-ni Atma-Katha' (Gujarati)
S B II–1 (Nov 1964) 31–35
On Jehangir's patronage and interest in Painting.

MAHFUZ'UL HAQ, M.   793
    'Discovery of a Portion of the Original Illustrated Ms. of
    Tārikh-i-Alfī written for the Emperor Akbar'
IsC V-3 (July 1931)

MAHFUZ'UL HAQ, M.   794
    '(The) Khān-i-Khānan and His Painters, Illuminators and
    Calligraphists'
IsC V-4 (Oct 1931) 621–30, 1 pl
Very useful article on painters and others patronised by Abdur-Rahim
Khan-i-Khanan

MAREK, J. & KNIZKOVA, H.   795
    '(The) Jenghis Khan Miniatures from the Court of Akbar the
    Great' (tr. by O. Kuthanova)
(London 1963) 36 Mughal miniatures

MEHTA, N. C.   796
    'Red Lilies, A Newly Discovered Mansūr'
Rupam Calcutta Nos. 19-20 (1924)

MOTICHANDRA   797
    'An Illustrated Ms. of the Dārāb-Nāmah'
BPOW No. 10 (1967) 32–42, 8 pls

MOTICHANDRA   798
'Portrait of Tansen'
QJNCPA III-1 (March 1974) 1-3
On its correct identification; also see No. 800 below

MOTICHANDRA   799
'(The) White Elephant'
LK Nos. 1-2 (April 1955-March 1956) 96, 1 colour pl.
Miniature Painting of late Akbar or early Jahangir period c. 1600-1610 A. D.

MOTICHANDRA & KHANDALAVALA, KARL J.   800
'A Contemporary Portrait of Tansen'
LK Nos- 1-2 (April 1955-March 1956) 11-21, 4 pls & 4 figs
Correct identification of the Portrait of Tansen; Hiren Mukherjee's Note in the **LK**
No. 14 (1969) 57, 2 pls, may also be considered in this connection

NAFICY, NOUCHINE   801
'Persian Contribution to Mughal Art'
II VII-4 (Dec 1954) 39-41
A small but interesting article

NAZIR AHMAD   802
·Jahangir's Album of Art : Muraqqā-i-Gulshan & its two
     Ādil Shāhi Paintings'
II XXX. 1-2 (March-June 1977) 25-43, 1 pl
A very learned and useful article

NAZIR AHMAD   803
(The) Mughal Artist Farrukh Beg'
IsC XXXV-2 (April 1961)

NIVEDITA, SISTER   804
'Notes on Paintings'
(The Passing of Shah Jehan, Shah Jehan dreaming of
     Taj, etc.)
JISOA Golden Jubilee No. (1961) pp. 106, 106-8, 108, 108-9 etc

PHILLOTT, D. C. & SHIRAZI, K.   805
'Notes on Certain Shi'ah Tilisms'
JASB 2nd Series II (1906) 534-37
A useful reference; Tilism miniatures have been done by Akbar's painters

PLOTINUS   806
'(The) Illustrations of the Romance of Amīr Hamzāh :
     A Review'
Rupam No. 29 (Jan 1927) 22-25

PRAMOD CHANDRA   807
'A Series of Ramayana Paintings of the Popular Mughal
School'
BPOW No. 6 (1958-59) 64-70

PRAMOD CHANDRA   808
'Ustad Salivahana and the Development of Popular Mughal
Art'
LK No. 8 (Oct 1960) 25-46, 44 pls (1 colour)
ViJnaptipatṛa of 1610 A. D., Shalibhadra-Charita of 1624 and other miniatures
of the period 1610-25; a very learned enumeration of the popular Mughal Art

PRAMOD CHANDRA & SHERMAN, E. LEE   809
'Tuti-Namah of the Cleveland Museum'
Transactions of the International Congress of Orientalists
XXVI-3, 728-30
One of the Earliest sets of Akbari paintings

RAI KRISHNADAS   810
'Akbar-Kalin Chitrit Grantha aur unke Chitrakar' (Hindi)
Kala-Nidhi Banares, I-3 with pls
Discusses authoritatively the illustrated mss. of the Akbar period, specifically
stylistic peculiarities and indigenous elements in the Hamzā-Nāmah

RANDHAWA, M. S.   811
'Paintings of the Babur-Namah'
Roop-Lekha XLII. 1-2 (1973) 9-16 & 5 pls
A useful survey

SANFORD, DAVID T.   812
'Identification of three Miniatures in the Nasli and A¹ice
Heeramaneck Collection'
AA XXXII-1 (1970) 42-48, 3 pls
One Rajasthani c. 1540 and two Mughal c. 1590; a very interesting study of the
miniatures; the third one depicts a tree-house throne with a winged deity, some-
thing related to the mysterious Pauranic beliefs which were prevalent in the 16th
century

SARASWATI, KUMAR   813
'Birds in Mughal Art'
Marg II-2 (Jan 1948) 29-41, 15 pls
From the Mughal miniatures of Akbar and Jehangir period

SEN, B.   814
'The Precursors of the Mughal School of Painting'
Roop–Lekha I-2 (1940) 49-53

SEN, GEETI   815
'Music & Musical Instruments in the Paintings of
Akbar-Nāmah'
QJNCPA VIII-4 (Dec 1979) 1-7

SINGH, CHANDRAMANI   816
'European Themes in Early Mughal Miniatures'
CHHAVI (1971) 401-10 with pls

SKELTON, ROBERT   817
'A Decorative Motif in Mughal Art'
in **'Aspects of Indian Art'** *(ed. P. Pal) (Brill Leiden 1972) 147-52, 12 pls*
Stylistic floral design used in Mughal Painting and Architecture

SKELTON, ROBERT   818
'Murshidabad Painting'
Marg X-1 (Dec 1956) 10-22, 15 pls
18th century miniature paintings of Bengal with apparent Mughal influence

SMART, ELLEN   819
'Four Illustrated Mughal Babur-Namah Mss.'
Art & Archaeology Research Papers No. 3 (London June 1973)

SOLOMON, W. E. GLADSTONE   820
'Colour and the Moghals'
IsC III-3 (July 1929)

SOLOMON, W. E. GLADSTONE   821
'Jehangir and his Artists'
IsC III-1 (Jan 1929)

SOLOMON, W. E. GLADSTONE   822
'Masterpieces of Moghul Painting'
IsC IV-1 (Jan 1930) 144-50

SOLOMON, W. E. GLADSTONE   823
'Mughal Pictures in London'
IsC XII-3 (July 1938)

SOLOMON, W. E. GLADSTONE   824
    'Perspective & the Mughals'
IsC V–4 (Oct 1931) 582-87
On an interesting aspect of Mughal Painting

SOLOMON, W. E. GLADSTONE   825
    '(The) Picture in the East and the West'
IsC XI-1 (Jan 1937) 146-49
Medieval painting as compared to its European counterpart

TASNEEM AHMED   826
    'Nādiru'l-Asr Mansūr (Ustād Mansūr Naqqāsh)'
II XXV-1 (March 1972) 51-55

TITLEY, NORAH   827
    'Miniature Paintings Illustrating the Works of Amir Khusrau'
Marg XXVIII-3 (June 1975) 19-52, 51 pls (including colour)

TYULAYEV, S. I.   828
    'Miniatures from a 16th century Ms : Bābur-Nāmah'
Marg XI–3 (June 1958) 45-48, 22 pls

VERMA, S. P.   829
    'Depiction of Trees in Akbari Illustrations'
II XXVIII (1975) 83-86, 4 pls

VERMA, S. P.   830
    'Mughal Painter's Aesthetic'
QRHS XV-2 (1975-76) 98-101

VERMA, S. P.   831
    'Painters from the 'Āīn-i-Akbarī'
II XXXII. 1-2 (March-June 1979) 19-29

VERMA, S. P.   832
    'Portraits of the Calligraphers Depicted in the Mughal
    Miniatures : A Historical Study'
IsC LIV-3 (July 1980) 173-86
Text 6 1/2 pages, references 7 1/2 pages, pls 4; In any case a useful article

VERMA, S. P.   833
    'Wine Pots at the Mughal Court in the 16th Century'
MIAM III (1975) 67–79, 7 pls showing 65 pots
An interesting and useful article

WELCH, STUART C. 834

'Early Mughal Miniatures from two Private Collections'
Ars Orientalis Vol. 3 (1959) 136-37 & pls
Also see the author's 'Mughal & Deccani Miniatures in an American Private Collection' in its Vol. 5 (1962) No. 5

WELCH, STUART C. 835

'Miniatures from a Ms. of the Dīwān-i-Hāfiz'
Marg XI-3 (June 1958) 56-62, 13 pls
On a set of paintings of Akbar's period

WELCH, STUART C. 836

'(The) Paintings of Basāwan'
LK No. 10 (Oct 1961) 7-17, 20 excellent pls (1 colour)
A very learned and useful article; the author also refers to Dr. W. Stande's articles on the subject particularly his 'Basawan' in the 'Encyclopaedia of World Art' (New York 1960) Vol. 2, 385-87

WIENER, ERNST COHN 837

'Miniatures from a Razm Nāmah'
Marg XI-3 (June 1958) 63-64, 4 pls

WILKINSON, J. V. S. 838

'A Dated Illustrated Ms. of Akbar's Reign'
JISOA II (1934) 67-69

5

MINIATURE PAINTING
(E) Rajput
(Dhoondhar, Mewar, Marwar, Bundi and other
Styles of Medieval Rajasthan)

BOOKS

ARCHER, W. G.   839
    'Indian Painting from Bundi and Kotah'
(London 1959) 56 pls

ARCHER, W. G.   840
    'Rajasthani Paintings from Shri Gopi Krishna Kanoria
       Collection'
(Calcutta 1962)
Originally published as 'Indian Paintings from Rajasthan: A Catalogue of
the G. K. Kanoria Exhibition' (Arts Council of Great Britain London 1957)

ARCHER, W. G. & BINNEY, E.   841
    'Rajput Miniatures from the Collection of Edwin Binney 3rd'
(Exhibition Catalogue Portland Museum, Portland Oregon 1968)

BEACH, MILO C.   842
    'Rajput and Related Paintings' in
    'The Arts of India and Nepal : The Nasli and Alice
       Heeramaneck Collection'
(Museum of Fine Arts Boston 1966)

BEACH, MILO C.   843
    'Rajput Painting at Bundi and Kotah'
(Boston 1974) pp. 72, 131 pls
Also published in **AA** XXXVI-3 Supplementa 1974

COOMARASWAMY, A. K.   **844**

'Catalogue of the Indian Collections in the Museums of Fine
Arts Boston' Parts I–VI

(Cambridge Mass. 1926) Parts I, II, V & VI on Rajput Painting

The basic and Classical work on the subject, indispensable for research

COOMARASWAMY, A. K.   **845**

'History of Indian and Indonesian Art'

(New Delhi 1972) with pls

Its Part—IV pp. 92-140 deals with Medieval and Rajput Painting; a classical
enumeration

COOMARASWAMY, A. K.   **846**

'Rajput Painting'

2 vols

*(London 1916; reprinted Motilal Banarsidass Delhi 1976, Foreword by
Karl J. Khandalavala)*

Being an account of the Hindu Paintings of Rajasthan and the Punjab Himalayas
from the 16th to the 19th century

DICKINSON, ERIC   **846—A**

'Kishangarh Paintings'

(Lalit Kala Akademi New Delhi 1959)

GANGOLY, O. C.   **847**

'Masterpieces of Rajput Painting'

(Calcutta 1926) 54 pls

Rajput and Pahari miniatures

GOETZ, H.   **848**

'(The) Art & Architecture of Bikaner State'

(Bruno Cassirer, Oxford 1950)

Authoritatively deals with the 'Painting in Bikaner' pp. 97-120; exquisitely
produced colour pls

GOSWAMI, PREMCHAND (ed)   **849**

'Rajasthan ki Laghu Chitra Shailiyan' (Hindi)

Part—I

(Rajasthan Lalit Kala Academy Jaipur 1972)

Collection of articles on various styles of Rajput Painting by Kunwar Sangram
Singh, Ramgopal Vijayavargiya, Mohanlal Gupta and others, with a number of
colour pls

GRAY, BASIL   850
  'Rajput Painting'
(*London 1948*)

GRAY, BASIL   851
  'Treasures of Indian Miniatures in the Bikaner Palace
    Collection'
(*Oxford 1955*)

JACOB, S. S.   852
  'Jeypore Portfolio of Architectural Details'
  12 vols
(*London 1890–1913; reprinted BPH Delhi–Varanasi 1977, first six vols*)
Its vols. VII, IX and X have coloured pls of Mural paintings (e. g. of dados) and
short notes

KHANDALAVALA, KARL J. (ed.)   853
  'Portfolio of Mewar Painting'
(*Lalit Kala Akademi New Delhi 1971*)

KHANDALAVALA, KARL J. & DICKINSON, ERIC   854
  'Kishangarh Painting'
(*Lalit Kala Akademi New Delhi 1959*) *with pls*
Reviewed in the LK No. 6 (April 1959) 82-90 and No. 8 (Oct 1960) 75-78

LEE, SHERMAN E.   855
  'Rajput Painting'
(*Cleveland New York 1960*)
A beautiful catalogue

MOTICHANDRA   856
  'Mewar Painting in the 17th century'
(*Lalit Kala Akademi New Delhi 1957*) *10 colour pls*

PAL, P.   857
  'Classical Tradition in Rajput Painting'
(*New York 1978*) *pp. 210, 78 pls*

PRAMOD CHANDRA 858
'Bundi Painting'
(*Lalit Kala Akademi New Delhi 1959*) *with 10 colour pls*

RANDHAWA, M. S. 858-A
'Indian Miniature Painting'
(*New Delhi 1981*) *pp. 128, 80 pls*

RAWSON, PHILIP 859
'(The) Art of Tantra'
(*Vikas London 1973, 1978*) *pp. 216, 189 pls*
Also deals with miniatures of the medieval styles Rajput Pahari etc which are not normally discussed on account of their sex contents

REIFF, R. 860
'Indian Miniatures : The Rajput Painters'
(*Rutland, Vermont 1959*)

SANGRAM SINGH, KUNWAR 861
'Dhundhar Painting'
(*Jaipur n. d.*)
Exhibition of Dhundhar Paintings from 16th to early 20th century organised on the occasion of 250th year of the foundation of the Jaipur City; includes Mural and miniature paintings of Amer Jaipur and adjoining thikanas

SATYA PRAKASH 861—A
'Rajasthani Miniatures'
(*Lalit Kala Akademi Jaipur 1958*)
Catalogue brought out on the eve of the exhibition of Rajasthani Miniatures at Mt. Abu

SATYA PRAKASH 861—B
'Rajasthani Paintings'
(*Lalit Kala Akademi Jaipur 1957*)
Catalogue brought out on the eve of the Exhibition of Rajasthan Paintings Jaipur

SHARMA, O. P. 862
'Indian Miniature Painting'
(*Brussels 1974*)
Mostly Rajput miniatures

SRIVASTAVA, V. S.   863
    'Catalogue & Guide to Ganga Golden Jubilee Museum,
    Bikaner'
(*Jaipur 1961*) *with pls*
Painting Section (pp. 27-41) lists portraits and miniatures of Bikaner and other schools, with a very useful introduction

VIJAYAVARGIYA, R. G.   864
    'Rajasthani Chitra-Kala' (Hindi)
(*Jaipur 1953*)

—   865
    'Art Treasures from the Sardar Museum Jodhpur'
(*Jaipur n. d.*) *with pls*
References to miniature paintings of various Rajput styles

—   866
    'Catalogue and Guide to Government Museum Alwar'
(*Jaipur 1961*) *with pls*
A separate section on paintings and mss. (pp. 56-104); lists hundreds of miniatures of Alwar, Mughal and Company schools.

—   867
    'Catalogue and Guide to Sardar Museum Jodhpur'
(*Jaipur 1961*) *with pls*
'Painting Section' (10-26) catalogues miniatures of the museum mainly of Jodhpur and Mewar styles

—   868
    . 'Catalogue and Guide to State Museum Bharatpur (Rajasthan)'
(*Jaipur 1961*) *with pls*
Valuable references to Portrait and Miniature paintings (preserved in the Museum) of various styles

—   869
    'Catalogue Government Museum Kota'
(*Jaipur 1961*) *with pls*
'Paintings Section' (pp. 13-24) catalogues miniatures mainly of Bundi Kotah and Mewar styles

—   870
    'Handbook to Victoria Hall Museum, Udaipur'
(*Jaipur 1961*) *with pls*
Catalogues miniatures of Mewar School of Painting on Bhāgawata, Rāmāyaṇa, Rasikapriyā, Gīta-Govinda, Rāga-Mālā, etc (pp. 22-25)

ARTICLES

AGARWAL, V. S. 871
'Rajasthani Chitrakala' (Hindi)
RB IV Nos. 2-3 (July-October 1954) 3-10
A very learned yet a simple and readable article

AGRE, JAGAT VIR SINGH 872
'Depiction of Landscape in Rajasthani Miniature Painting
(13th-17th century)'
PRHC IX (Kota 1976) 58-61
A brief appraisal only

ANDHARE, S. K. 873
'Painting from the Thikana of Deogarh'·
BPOW No. 10 (1967) 43-53, 13 pls
In Mewar (Rajasthan) during the first quarter of the 19th century

ANDHARE, SHRIDHAR 874
'Three New Documents of the Reign of Rana Sangram Singh
of Mewar (A. D. 1710-34)'
LK No. 19 (1979) 60, 5 pls
Miniature paintings of Gita-Govinda, Bihari-Satsai etc

ARCHER, W. G. 875
'General Survey of Rajasthani Styles : Kotah'
Marg XI-2 (March 1958) 65-67, 4 pls

ARCHER, W. G. 876
'(The) Problems of Bikaner Paintings'
Marg V-1 (Dec 1951) 8-16, 7 pls of miniatures and 5 of epigraphs

BANERJI, ADRIS 877
'Schools of Rajasthani Paintings'
IMB II-2 (July 1967) 50-55

BEACH, MILO CLEVELAND 878
'Painting of the Later 18th century at Bundi and Kotah'
In 'Aspects of Indian Art' (ed. by P. Pal)
(Brill Leiden 1972) 124-29, 9 pls

BEACH, MILO CLEVELAND   879
    'Rajput Painting at Bundi and Kota'
AA XXXVI-3 (Supplementa, 1974)
Also published in Book-Form (Boston 1974)

BINYON, LAWRENCE   880
    'Relations between Rajput and Moghul Painting :
    A New Document'
RUPAM No. 29 (Jan 1927) 4-5

CHAGHTAI, M. A.   881
    '(A) Few Hindu Miniature Painters of the 18th and
    19th centuries'
AIOC VI (Patna 1930) 233-39

CHAKRAVARTI, P. L. & SOMANI, R. V.   882
    'Mewar Shaili ka prachintam (V. S. 1286 ka) Rekhankan'
    (Hindi)
SP XXV-1 (Jan-March 1974) 53-54
Carved figures in the Samādhīśvara Temple at Chittorgarh with dated inscriptions V. S. 1286/1229 A. D.; it is very doubtful if these can be deemed paintings as Radha Krishna Vashishta tried to brand them vide his article in the **SP** XXVI-1 (Jan-March 1975) 66-67

CHATTERJEE, S. K.   883
    'Masterpiece of Rajput Painting : A Review'
RUPAM No. 30 (April 1927) 54-58

CHOYAL, PARMANAND   884
    'Rajasthani Chitrakala ki Prashthabhumi' (Hindi)
SP XVII, 1-2 (Jan-April 1966) 100-112
An interesting survey of Rajasthani Painting

CHOYAL, S. M.   885
    'Badhera-Bilada ke Rajasthani-Chitra' (Hindi)
RB V-2 (November 1956) 83-89
Catalogues three collections of the Bilada Thikana of 47, 54 and 87 miniature paintings: important information

DAS, A. K.   886
    'Homage to Jaipur : Miniatures'
Marg XXX-4 (Sept 1977) 77-94, 18 excellent pls (10 colour)
A useful article on the miniature painting of Jaipur

DICKINSON, ERIC 887
    'General Survey of Rajasthani Styles : Kishangarh'
Marg XI-2 (March 1958) 60-61, 2 pls

DICKINSON, ERIC 888
    '(The) Way of Pleasure : The Kishangarh Paintings'
Marg III-4 (Sept 1950) 29-35

DOSHI, SARYU 889
    'An Illustrated Ms. from Aurangabad Dated 1650 A. D.'
LK No. 15 (1972) 19-28, 7 pls (1 colour)
Found at Udaipur (Rajasthan); belongs to the Mewar style

DWIVEDI, V. P. 890
    'Some Inscribed and Dated Rajasthani Miniatures in the
       Collection of State Museum Lucknow'
JISOA New Series VIII (1976-77) 48-56

GANGOLY, A. N. 891
    'A Vaishnavite Miniature from Udaipur'
RUPAM No. 30 (April 1927) 61

GANGOLY, O. C. 892
    'Acquisitions of Rajput Miniatures'
BMB XIV (1962) 9-16

GANGOLY, O. C. 893
    'A Group of Vallabhacharya or Nathdwara Paintings'
BMB I-2 (Feb-July 1944) 31-46
With an appendix by Hermann Goetz

GANGOLY, O. C. 894
    'Rajasthani Portraits'
Marg XI-2 (March 1958) 22-24, 3 pls
Of the Rajput style

GHOSH, D. P. 895
    'Orissan Painting'
JISOA IX (1941) 194-200

GOETZ, H. 896

'An Illustrated Early Rajput Ms.'
D. V. Potdar Com. Vol. (ed. by S. N. Sen) Poona (1950)
82–87 and pls

GOETZ, H. 897

'(The) First Golden Age of Udaipur : Rajput Art
in Mewar during the Period of Mughal Supremacy'
Ars Orientalis II (1957) 427–37 & pls; reprinted **RAA** *95–106 and 26 pls*
Deals with the development of Mewar Painting

GOETZ, H. 898

'General Survey of Rajasthani Styles : Bikaner'
Marg XI-2 (March 1958) 62–64, 5 pls

GOETZ, H. 899

'General Survey of Rajasthani Styles : Jaipur'
Marg XI-2 (March 1958) 53–59, 12 pls

GOETZ, H. 900

'General Survey of Rajasthani Styles : Marwar'
Marg XI-2 (March 1958) 42–49, 28 pls

GOETZ, H. 901

'General Survey of Rajasthani Styles : Mewar
Marg XI-2 (March 1958) 38–41, 4 pls

GOETZ, H. 902

'(The) Kachhwaha School of Rajput Painting'
(Amber and Jaipur)
BMB IV (Aug 1946–July 1947) 33–48
An excellent article with 20 pls; reprinted **RAA** 68-82 and pls

GOETZ, H. 903

'(The) Marwar School of Painting'
BMB V (1947-48) 43–54. 15 pls; reprinted **RAA** *83–94 & pls;
also in the* **MARG** *Rajasthani Paintings Vol. XI-2 (March 1958)
42–49 with pls*

GOETZ, H.   **904**
'New Discoveries of Rajput Painting'
IAL XXI (1947) 40-41

GOETZ, H.   **905**
'(A) New Key to Early Rajput and Indo-Muslim Painting'
Roop-Lekha XXIII (1952) 1-16

GOETZ, H.   **906**
'Notes on Some Schools of Rajput Painting'
JISOA V (1937) 159-66

GOETZ, H.   **907**
'Notes on the Vallabhacharya Paintings
from Udaipur and Jodhpur in the Baroda State Museum'
BMB 1-2 (1944) 41-46

GOETZ, H. & KHANDALAVALA, KARL J.   **908**
'(The) Problem of the Classification and Chronology of
Rajput Painting and the Bikaner Miniatures : A Controversy'
Marg V-1 (Dec 1951) 17-22
Correspondence on an important problem

GOETZ, H.   **909**
'Rajasthani Chitra Kala me Nagaur Shaili' (Hindi)
Kala-Nidhi Banares I-2, 82-90 ; also in the AA XII. 1-2
On Nagaur School Painting

GOETZ, H.   **910**
'Rajput Art : Its Problems'
RAA (Wiesbaden 1978) 23-30
On the sources and development of Rajput Painting

GOETZ, H.   **911**
'Rajput School'
Originally published in the **Encyclopaedia of World Art** *XI (1966)
822-39; published in the* **RAA** *(Rajput Art & Architecture ed. J. Jain
and J. J. Neubauer, Wiesbaden 1978) 1-22 & illustrations*
On various aspects of Rajput painting

GOSWAMI, B. N.   912
        'Toda-Gashia : Painting at the Scindia's Court at
        Gwalior'
Art Heritage No. 2 (n. d.) 7–21, 14 pls
On the 19th century paintings of Gwalior

HANDIQUI, K. K.   913
        '(The) Naishadha-Charita and Rajput Painting'
IHQ XII-3 (1936) 526-29

HENDLEY, T. H.   914
        'Decorative Art in Rajputana'
Journal of Indian Art London II (1888) 43-50, 9 pls
(7 coloured)

JAVALIA, B. M.   915
        'Madhyakaleen Chitra-Karma men Prayukta Rangon ki
        Nirman-Vidhi' (Hindi)
VB XX. 3-4 (July-Dec 1977) 61-63
Preparation of colours in Medieval Painting

KHAJANCHI, MOTICHAND   916
        'Bikaner ki Chitrakala' (Hindi)
RB V-1 (January 1956) 52-54, 6 pls
A Small but interesting article

KHANDALAVALA, KARL J.   917
        'A Group of Bundi Miniatures'
BPOW No. 3 (1952-53) 25-35, with pls

KHANDALAVALA, KARL J   918
        'Five Bundi Paintings of the Late 17th Century A. D.'
BPOW No. 5 (1955-1957) 50–56 with pls

KHANDALAVALA, KARL J.   919
        'Leaves from Rajasthan'
Marg IV-3 (June 1951) 1-24 & 49-56 and pls

KHANDALAVALA, KARL J.   920
        'Problem of Rajasthani Painting : The Origin and
        Development of Rajasthani Painting'
Marg XI-2 (March 1958) 4-17, 20 pls
A very learned and useful article

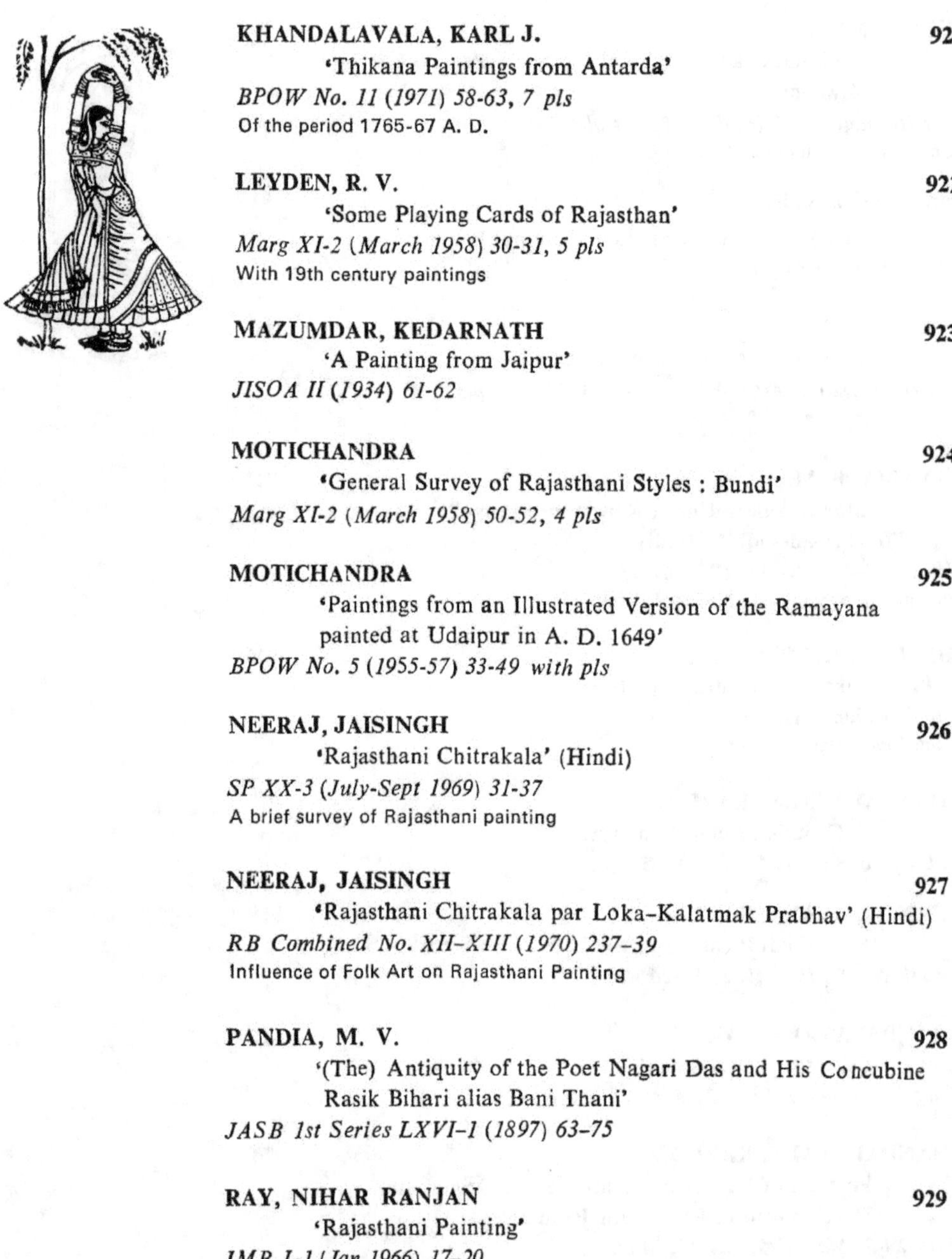

KHANDALAVALA, KARL J.   921
'Thikana Paintings from Antarda'
BPOW No. 11 (1971) 58-63, 7 pls
Of the period 1765-67 A. D.

LEYDEN, R. V.   922
'Some Playing Cards of Rajasthan'
Marg XI-2 (March 1958) 30-31, 5 pls
With 19th century paintings

MAZUMDAR, KEDARNATH   923
'A Painting from Jaipur'
JISOA II (1934) 61-62

MOTICHANDRA   924
'General Survey of Rajasthani Styles : Bundi'
Marg XI-2 (March 1958) 50-52, 4 pls

MOTICHANDRA   925
'Paintings from an Illustrated Version of the Ramayana
painted at Udaipur in A. D. 1649'
BPOW No. 5 (1955-57) 33-49 with pls

NEERAJ, JAISINGH   926
'Rajasthani Chitrakala' (Hindi)
SP XX-3 (July-Sept 1969) 31-37
A brief survey of Rajasthani painting

NEERAJ, JAISINGH   927
'Rajasthani Chitrakala par Loka–Kalatmak Prabhav' (Hindi)
RB Combined No. XII–XIII (1970) 237–39
Influence of Folk Art on Rajasthani Painting

PANDIA, M. V.   928
'(The) Antiquity of the Poet Nagari Das and His Concubine
Rasik Bihari alias Bani Thani'
JASB 1st Series LXVI–1 (1897) 63–75

RAY, NIHAR RANJAN   929
'Rajasthani Painting'
IMB I-1 (Jan 1966) 17-20
Gives a useful appraisal

REU, B. N.   930
'(The) Picture Gallery of the Jodhpur Museum'
Journal of Indian Museums IV (1948) 41 ff.

SATYA PRAKASH   931
'Rajasthan men Chitrakala ka Kramik Vikas' (Hindi)
RB VIII. 1-2 (March 1963) 9-19, 4 pls
Though mainly devoted to the evolution of Miniature painting, the article also
alludes to Mural paintings of Amer, Chittor and Kumbhalgarh

SATYA PRAKASH   931-A
'Rajasthani Chitrakala ki Kishangarh Shaili men Krishna
  ka bhavankan' (Hindi)
Marubharati Pilani II-1, (February 1954) 26-28

SATYA PRAKASH   931-B
'Rajasthani Chitrakala ki Jaipur Shaili-Punaravalokana'
  (Hindi)
'Agama-Sahitya men varnita Kala-Samagri' (Hindi)
'Silpa-Ratna men varnita Chitra-kala Samagri' (Hindi)
Akriti Jaipur I Nos. 10-12 (May 1967) 38-41, 33-34 and II-3 (Jan 1968)
3-5 respectively

SENGUPTA, B. K.   932
'Some Types of Nayika in Rajput Painting'
AIOC XIX (Delhi 1957) 160; also published in the **Journal of the**
Gauhati University *IX (1958) (Arts) 147-49*

SHAH, U. P.   933
'A Page from an Illustrated Ms. Rati-Rahasya'
BMB XXIII (1971) 11-14, 2 pls

SOMANI R. V.   934
'Gangrar Gaon men khudi 14-veen Shatabdi ki
  Akritiyan' (Hindi)
SP XXVII-4 (Oct-Dec 1976) 41-42
14th century carved figures at Gangrar; these incised figures are with epigraphs;
whether these can be called painting and included as such is open to study

SOMANI, R. V.   935
'Ghanerao ki Chitrankana—Parampara' (Hindi)
VB XXI-4 (Oct-Dec 1978) 12-13
Miniature style of Ghanerao (Pali) 18th-19th centuries

SOMANI, R. V.   936
    'Jahajpur ka V. S. 1382 ka ek Rekhankan' (Hindi)
SP XXVIII-2 (April-June 1977) 41-42;
Incised figure of horse (1325 A. D.); it is a painting in the author's view

VASHISHTHA, RADHAKRISHNA   937
    'Mewar ke Prarambhik Chitravashesh tatha unka
        Kalavadi Vishleshana' (Hindi)
SP XXV. 3-4 (July-Dec 1974) 77-80
A small essay on Mewar Painting giving a hurried survey only

VASHISHTHA, RADHAKRISHNA   938
    'Mewar ksetra ke Prachintam Chitravashesh' (Hindi)
SP XX-3 (July-Sept 1969) 55-61
Ancient remains of painting of Mewar; also refers to the medieval painting of
Mewar

VASHISHTHA, RADHAKRISHNA   939
    'Paramparagat Mewar Chitra Shaili ke kala Tatvon men
        Adhunik Chitrakala ke Prerak Tatva' (Hindi)
SP XXVIII-2 (April-June 1977) 35-37
On the mewar Painting; much of what he writes awaits intensive study

VASHISHTHA, RADHAKRISHNA   940
    'Rajasthani Chitrakala men Mewar Shaili ki Pramukh
        Upalabdhiyan' (Hindi)
SP XXVII-3 (July-Sept 1976) 46-56
On the various styles of Mewar Painting

VASHISHTHA, RADHAKRISHNA   941
    'Rangon ka Manovaijnanik Drshtakon evam Mewar
        Chitra Shaili' (Hindi)
SP XXVIII-1 (Jan-March 1977) 58-61
A subjective interpretation of Psychological meaning of colours in Mewar
miniatures

VATSYAYAN, KAPILA   942
    'An Illustrated Ms. of the Gita-Govinda from Mewar'
JISOA New Series Dr Motichandra Com. Vol. (1978) 38-59
A very learned and useful article on Mewar Painting

VATSYAYAN, KAPILA   943
    'Some Aspects of North Indian Dance as seen in
        Paintings of the Late Medieval Period'
AIOC XXII (Gauhati 1965) 203

—⋅◆⋅—

5

MINIATURE PAINTING

(F) Pahari

(Kangra, Chamba, Guler, Basohli, Mankot, Nalagarh, Garhwal and other Hill Centres of Miniature Art of Jammu-Kashmir, the Punjab, H. P. and U. P. including Painting under the Sikhs)

BOOKS

ARCHER, W. G.   **944**
    'Garhwal Painting'
    (with Introduction and Notes)
(*London 1954*)

ARCHER, W. G.   **945**
    'Indian Paintings from the Punjab Hills' 2 vols
(*London 1952; revised and reprinted OUP Delhi 1973*)
Excellently reviewed by Khandalavala in the **LK** No. 18, 51-55; review itself
gives complete enumeration of the subject; also reviewed by Motichandra in
the **Marg** VI-1 (Dec 1952) 22-27 with 7 pls

ARCHER, W. G.   **946**
    'Kangra Painting'
    (with Introduction and Notes)
(*London 1952*)
Reviewed excellently by Karl J. Khandalavala in the **Marg** VI-3 (June 1953)
25-31 with 7 pls; the review itself is an article on the subject

ARCHER, W. G.   **947**
    'Paintings of the Sikhs'
(*London 1966*)

ARYAN, K. C.   **948**
    'Punjab Painting' (1841-1941)
(*New Delhi*)

FRENCH, G. C.　　　　949
'Himalayan Art'
(*London 1931*)

GOETZ, H.　　　　950
'Studies in the History and Art of Kashmir and Indian
Himalaya'
(*Wiesbaden 1969*)

GOSWAMY, B. N.　　　　951
'Pahari Paintings of the Nala-Damayanti Theme'
(*Delhi 1975*)
A Collection of paintings of unknown Pahari artists of the second half of the
18th century A. D.

GOSWAMY, B. N.　　　　952
'Painters at the Sikh Court-A Study of Twenty Documents'
(*Wiesbaden 1975*)
On the painters of Guler who later worked for Sikh Chieftains

GUPTA, S. N.　　　　953
'Catalogue of Paintings in the Central Museum Lahore'
(*Calcutta 1922*)

HANDA. O. C.　　　　954
'Pahari Folk Art'
(*Taraporevala Bombay 1975*) pp. 84, 49 pls (including Colour) and 49 figs
A learned treatise on the subject

KHANDALAVALA, KARL J. (ed.)　　　　955
'(The) Bhagawata-Purana in Kangra Painting'
(*Lalit Kala Akademi Portfolio No. 14, New Delhi 1965*)
Reviewed in LK No. 18, 43-44

KHANDALAVALA, KARL J.　　　　956
'Pahari Miniature Painting'
(*Bombay 1958*)

LAWRENCE, GEORGE　　　　957
'Indian Art—Paintings of the Himalaya State'
(*London*)

MUKANDI LAL　　　　958
'Garhwal Painting'
(*New Delhi 1968*) pp. 110, 68 pls (31 colour)
Reviewed by Khandalavala in the LK 15 (1972) 58-59

RANDHAWA, M. S.   959
    'Basohli Painting'
(Delhi 1959) pp 126, 43 pls (38 colour)
Earliest centre of Pahari style combining the ancient tradition of Folk Art with
the Mughal; Reviewed ably in the **LK** 8 (Oct 1960) 81-83; further correspondence in the **LK** No. 9 (April 1961) 60-62 which throws valuable light on the
subject

RANDHAWA, M. S. & BHAMBRI, S. D.   959-A
    'Basohli Paintings of the Rasamanjari'
(Abhinav New Delhi 1981) Pp. xvi + 149, 87 pls
With Sanskrit and English trans

RANDHAWA, M. S.   960
    'Chamba Painting'
(Lalit Kala Akademi New Delhi 1967; reprinted 1975) 19 pls (11 colour)
Reviewed by Doughlas Barrett in the **LK** 14 (1969) 63-64

RANDHAWA, M. S.   961
    'Kangra Paintings of the Bhagawata Purana'
(Delhi 1960)

RANDHAWA, M. S.   962
    'Kangra Paintings of the Bihari Sat-Sai'
(National Museum New Delhi 1966)
Reviewed by Khandalavala in the **LK** 14 (1969) 60

RANDHAWA, M. S.   963
    'Kangra Paintings of the Gita-Govinda'
(National Museum New Delhi 1963)
Reviewed by Khandalavala in the **LK** No. 14 (1969) 60-61

RANDHAWA, M. S.   964
    'Kangra Paintings of Love'
(Delhi 1962) pp. 209, 114 pls (25 colour)
On theme of love as portrayed by Hindi poets like Keshavdas and Bihari

RANDHAWA, M. S.   965
    'Kangra Valley Painting'
(Delhi 1955) pp. 67 29 masterpieces of Kangra paintings
Latter part of the 18th century A. D.; reviewed in the **LK** 1-2 (April 1955-March
1956) 152-56 with 1 colour pl; Revised edition published by the Publication
Division (New Delhi 1972)

RANDHAWA, M. S.   966

'(The) Krishna Legend in Pahari Painting'
(*Lalit Kala Akademi New Delhi 1956*)

VOGEL, J. Ph.   967

'Catalogue of Bhuri Singh Museum Chamba'
(*Calcutta 1909*)
Of Pahari paintings

ARTICLES

ANAND KRISHNA   968

'(The) Vigour and Passion of Molaram'
(An interesting Dasa-Mahavidya Set from Garhwal)
Art Heritage No. 2 (n. d.) 23–29, 6 pls
18th century miniatures; 2 depict Shava—Sadhana (Tantric practices) and are
extremely interesting

ANAND, M. R.   969

'Painting under the Sikhs'
Marg VII-2 (March 1954) 23–31, 8 pls
19th century paintings of the Punjab

ANAND, M. R.   970

'(The) Pictorial Situation in Pahari Painting'
Marg XXI-4 (Sept 1968) 2–16, 15 pls (2 colour)
Excellent editorial to the Number

ANAND, M. R.   971

'Specimens of Paintings under the Sikhs'
Marg X-2 (March 1957) 37–44, 7 pls
19th century miniature paintings

ARCHER, W. G.   972

'(The) Master of the Kangra Bhāgawata Purāṇa'
*Roop-Lekha XXXVIII (M. S. Randhawa Presentation Vol.)
64–72, 6 pls*
On Randhawa's study of the Kangra Painting

ARCHER, W. G.   973
'Pahari Miniatures'
(A concise History)
Marg XXVIII-2 (March 1975) 2-44, 48 pls numerous colour
Special number of the miniature paintings of Mankot, Basohli, Kulu, Jammu,
Jasrota, Mandi, Suket, Nurpur, Chamba, Guler, Garhwal, Sirmur, Kangra etc

ARCHER, W. G.   974
'Problems of Painting in the Panjab Hills'
Marg X-2 (March 1957) 30-36, 8 pls

ARCHER, W. G. & RANDHAWA, M. S.   975
'Some Nurpur Painting : A Symposium'
Marg VIII-3 (June 1955) 8-25 and 25 pls
18th century and later paintings

BANERJI, ADRIS   976
'An Illustrated Hindi Manuscript of Sakuntala
Dated 1789 A.D.'
LK 1-2 (April 1955-March 1956) 46-54, 8 pls (1 colour)
Of the Kangra Style

BEACH, MILO C.   977
'A Bhagwata-Purana from the Punjab Hills'
*Bulletin of the Boston Museum of Fine Arts Boston LXIII No. 333
(1965) 168-77 & pls*

BHATIA, USHA   978
'Two Inscribed Portraits of Vaisnava Mahants from the
Chandigarh Museum'
LK No. 19 (1979) 58, 2 pls
Pahari style, early 18th century A. D.

BHATTACHARYYA, A. K.   979
'A Set of Kulu Folk Paintings in the National Museum of
India'
AA XX. 2-3 (1957) 165-183, 10 pls, 1 Map
18th century set; the article usefully describes and analyses the paintings

COOMARASWAMY, A. K.   980
'A Pastoral Paradise'
RUPAM No. 42-44 (April-Oct 1930) 14-16
About a Kangra Painting

FRENCH, J. C.   981
  'Samsarchand of Kangra'
IAL XXI (1947) 89-91

GANGOLY, O. C.   982
  'An Editio Princeps of Sundara-Srngara'
RUPAM No. 30 (1927) 47-51
Pahari Painting

GANGOLY, O C.   983
  'Garhwal Painting : A Review of Archer's Monograph'
Marg VIII-3 (June 1955) 32-37, 5 pls

GANGOLY, O. C.   984
  'Pahari Miniatures in Baroda Museum'
BMB X-XI (1953-55) 7-17

GANGOLY, O. C.   985
  '(The) Problem of Molaram'
Marg IV-4 (July 1950) 34-39, 5 pls (1 colour)
The famous Garhwal Painter

GANGOLY, O. C.   986
  '(A) Set of Ramayana Illustrations of Pahari School'
BMB IX (1952-53) 25-30

GANGOLY, O. C.   987
  '(The) Toilette of Radha : A Late Kangra Miniature'
RUPAM No. 29 (Jan 1927) 15

GHOSE, AJIT   988
  '(The) Basohli School of Rajput Painting'
RUPAM No. 37 (Jan 1929) 6-16

GHOSE, A.   989
  'Pahari Schools of Indian Painting'
Roop-Lekha XXVIII. 1-2 (1958) 34-44 & pls

GOETZ, H.   990
  'A Muslim Painting of the Kangra School'
BMB III-2 (Feb-July 1946) 41-45

GOETZ, H. 991

'(The) Antiquities of the Chamba State : An Art
Historical Outline'
*Journal of the U. P. Historical Society I. 1–2 (1953) 76–99, 5 pls;
reprinted in* **'Studies in the History and Art of Kashmir and the Indian
Himalaya'** *(Wiesbaden 1969) viii+197 pp. and 49 pls;*
Deals elaborately with Chamba and other styles of Pahari Painting

GOETZ, H. 992

'(The) Art of Chamba in the Islamic Period'
*JOI XI-2 (1961) 135–44, 9 figs and XI-3 (1962) 219–36, 18 figs;
reprinted in* **'Studies in the History and Art of Kashmir and the Indian
Himalaya'** *(Wiesbaden 1969)*

GOETZ, H. 993

'(The) Background of Pahari-Rajput Painting'
Roop-Lekha XXII-1 (1951) 1–16, 25 pls

GOETZ, H. 994

'Raja Ishwara Sen of Mandi and the History of Kangra
Painting'
BMB II-1 (1944-45) 35-38

GOETZ, H. 995

'Rajput Sculpture & Painting under Raja Umed Singh
of Chamba'
Marg VII-4 (Sept 1954) 23–34, 11 pls
Includes study of murals and miniatures, mid-18th century; reprinted **RAA**
138-43 & pls

GOETZ, H. 996

'Some Court Portraits of the Pahari School in Dutch
Collections'
JISOA I (1933) 120–23

GOSWAMY, B. N. 997

'(The) Artist Family of Rajol : New Light on an Old Problem'
Roop-Lekha XXXVI Nos. 1-2
On Pahari Miniature Painting

GOSWAMY, B. N. 998
'(The) Artist Ranjha and a Dated Set of Ramayana Drawings'
Chhavi I (1971) 224–31 with pls and figs.
19th century Pahari Painting

GOSWAMY, B. N. 999
'Of Patronage and Pahari Painting'
In 'Aspects of Indian Art' (ed. P. Pal, Brill Leiden 1972) 130-38, 8 pls

GOSWAMY, B. N. 1000
'On Two Portraits of Pahari Artists'
AA XXXIV. 2-3 (1972) 225-231, 5 pls
Manak and Khushala of Guler first half of the 18th century, Portraits in the
National Museum Delhi

GOSWAMY, B. N. 1001
'(The) Pahari Artists : A Study'
Roop-Lekha XXXII–2 (1961) 31-50 and pls

GOSWAMY, B. N. 1002
'Pahari Paintings of the Nala Damayanti Theme : Discussion
       in New Light'
Roop-Lekha XXXVIII (M. S. Randhawa Presentation Vol.)
85-108, 17 pls
Of the Period from 1763 to 1827 A. D.

GOSWAMY, B. N. 1003
'Pahari Painting : The Family as the Basis of Style'
Marg XXI-4 (Sept 1968) 16–62, 48 pls (4 colour)
The argument, the Clue, the Family and the Style; excellent visuals

GOSWAMY, B. N. 1004
'Painters in Chamba : A Discussion of the Attra Inscription'
LK No. 15 (1972) 39-42, 2 pls

GOSWAMY, B. N. 1005
'(The) Problem of the Artist Nainsukh of Jasrota'
AA XXVIII. 2-3 (1966) 205-210
Pahari Painter of Jammu of mid-18th century

GOSWAMY, B. N. & JHAMB, H. 1006
'(A) Unusual Series of Illustrations to the Bhagavadgita'
AA XXXVIII. 2-3 (1976) 158-166. 12 pls
Preserved in the Chandigarh Museum, basically of the Pahari school

GOSWAMY, KARUNA 1007
·(A) Pahari Painting of a Jagannath Temple'
Chhavi I (1971) 235-39 with pls

GOSWAMY, KARUNA 1008
'Two Pahari Illustrations of the Bhaktamaʻa'
Roop-Lekha XXXVIII (M. S. Randhawa Presentation Vol) 73-78, 2 pls
Two drawings of the last quarter of the 18th century preserved in the Chandigarh Museum

GUPTA, S. N. 1009
'(The) Sikh School of Painting'
Rupam No. 12 (1922) 125-28

KHANDALAVALA, KARL J. 1010
'Kangra Paintings from Bhāgwat-Puiāṇa in the Baroda
Museum'
BMB XIX (1966) 1-7

KHANDALAVALA, KARL J. 1011
'Krishna's Bath'
Marg I-2 (Jan 1947) 58, 1 colour pl
On a Pahari miniature

KHANDALAVALA, KARL J. 1012
'Notes on Pahari Painting'
LK No. 16 (1974) 37-47, 10 pls (1 colour)
On the Pahari miniatures of Jammu (18th-19th centuries) Guler (18th century)
Kangra (early 19th) Nurpur (first half of the 19th) etc

KHANDALAVALA, KARL J. 1013
'Three Pahari Drawings'
BPOW No. 12 (1973) 73-74, 3 pls
Datable to c.1700 to 1750

MEHTA, N. C. 1014
'Two Pahari Painters of Tehri Garhwal-Manaku and Chaitu·
RUPAM No. 26 (April 1926) 49-54

MISRA, K. P.   1015
    'An Illustrated Ms. of Madhu-Mālatī'
RUPAM Nos. 33-34 (1928) 9-11

MITTAL, JAGDISH   1016
    'An Early Guler Painting'
LK No. 11 (April 1962) 31-34, 5 pls (1 colour)
Mid-18th century

MITTAL, JAGDISH   1017
    'New Studies in Pahari Painting'
LK No. 12 (Oct 1962) 26-35, 23 pls
An extremely valuable paper on 18th century Chamba paintings; also deals with the artists

MITTAL, JAGDISH   1018
    'Pahari Chitra-kala ka Ankan Vidhan' (Hindi)
Kala-Nidhi Banares I-3
Interesting study of the technique of Pahari painting including colours and their preparation

MITTAL, JAGDISH   1019
    'Some Ramayana and Bhagwata Drawings of Chamba'
Marg VIII-3 (June 1955) 26-31, 6 pls of drawings

MOTICHANDRA & KHANDALAVALA, KARL J.   1020
    'An Aniruddha-Usha Series from Chamba and the
        Painter Ramlal'
LK 1-2 (April 1955-March 1956) 37-44, 4 pls (1 colour) & 2 figs
21 paintings of the period 1764-90

MUKANDI LAL   1021
    'Some Notes on Mola Ram'
RUPAM No. 8 (Oct 1921) 22-30
On the famous Pahari Painter Molaram

OHRI, V. C.   1022
    'Four Important Inscriptions on Pahari Paintings'
LK 11 (April 1962) 58-60

OHRI, V. C.   1023
    'Four Pahari Portraits'
LK No 14 (1969) 21-23, 5 pls
Three portraits of Raja Diwan Indra Dev Bandralta in Jammu, 18th century A. D.

OHRI, V. C.   1024
'Kangra Painting of Pre-Samsar Chand Period'
LK No, 17 (n. d.) 43, 2 pls
c. 1770 A. D.

OHRI, V. C.   1025
'Laharu and Mahesh the Miniature Painters at Chamba in the
mid-18th century A. D.'
LK No. 13 (1967) 50, 3 pls
Study from a wooden Toraṇa at Chamba

OHRI, V. C.   1026
'(The) Origins of Pahari Paintings'
Roop-Lekha XXXVIII. 1-2 (M. S. Randhawa Presentation Vol)
109-19, 20 pls
Deals elaborately with early style of Basohli, a very useful article

OHRI, V. C.   1027
'Paintings of the Mid–eighteenth Century from Guler'
LK No. 15 (1972) 54-55, 2 pls
Of Bhāgawat set in Basohli style done at Guler

PANWAR, S. S.   1028
'Garhwal Painting-Some Erroneous Impressions Corrected'
LK No. 19 (1979) 51-56, 7 pls
Related to the painter Molaram and other problems, a very interesting article

PAUL, SUWARCHA   1029
'Portrait of Bhagat Maluk Das'
LK No. 19 (1979) 59-60, 2 pls
Guler Painting dated 1809 A. D.

RANDHAWA, M. S.   1030
'Guler the Birth-Place of Kangra Painting'
Marg VI-4 (Dipavali 1953) 30-44, 20 excellent pls followed by a Note
on Guler Paintings by Khandalavala

RANDHAWA, M. S.   1031
'Kangra Artists'
Art & Letters XX-1 (1955) 1-9 and pls

RANDHAWA, M. S.   1032
'Kangra Painting'
Dr G. Yazdani Com. Vol. (Hyderabad 1966) 134-36, 5 pls

RANDHAWA, M. S.   1033
‘Manak : Painter of the Gita-Govinda Paintings-was he a
Garhwal Artist ?’
Roop-Lekha XXXI-2 (Dec 1960) 3-9, 4 pls
Manak migrated to Guler and Kangra and he did these paintings c. 1790 A. D.

RANDHAWA, M. S.   1034
‘(A) Note on Rasamanjarī Paintings from Basohli’
Roop-Lekha XXXI-1 (1960) 16-26

RANDHAWA, M. S.   1035
‘Paintings from Mankot’
LK No. 6 (April 1959) 72-75, 11 pls
In Jammu, of the period from 1650 to 1680, c. 1690 and c. 1740 A. D.

RANDHAWA, M. S.   1036
‘Paintings from Nalagarh’
LK 1-2 (April 1955-March 1956) 81-86, 7 pls 1 fig and 1 map
Painted during the period 1788—1857 A. D. in the Himachal Pradesh (Pahari
style)

RANDHAWA, M. S.   1037
‘Studies in Pahari Painting’
Roop-Lekha XLII. 1-2 (1973) 80-85
On how Coomaraswamy Archer and other scholars took up this study: a very
useful prelude

RANDHAWA, M. S.   1038
‘Sujanpur Tira : The Cradle of Kangra Art’
Marg VII-3 (June 1954) 21-36, 15 pls
A very detailed enumeration

SHARMA, O. P.   1039
‘Two Dated and Illustrated Pahari Mss. in the National
Museum New Delhi’
Roop-Lekha XXXVIII (M. S. Randhawa Presentation Vol.) 79-84, 8 pls
Dated 1776 and 1779 A. D. respectively; first is on Bhāgvata-Purāṇa, the second
has three texts : ‘Anvarachandrikā’ ‘Bihārī-Satsaī’ and ‘Rasarāja’ of Matiram

TREASURYVALA, B. N.   1040
‘A New Variety of Pahari Paintings’
JISOA XI (1943) 133-35

VASWANI, A. S.   **1041**

'Story of Dhruva Maharaja in Kangra Valley Paintings'
*IAL with numerous colour pls (no details of publication are available in
this copy)*

VOGEL, J. Ph   **1042**

'Portrait Painting in Kangra and Chamba'
AA X–3 (1947) 200–215, 6 pls
An excellent introductory article by one of the earliest art-historians, illustrated
with beautiful pls

—   **1043**

'Giri-Goverdhana-Dhāraṇa : A Kangra Miniature'
RUPAM No. 41 (Jan 1930) 16–18

5

MINIATURE PAINTING
(G) Deccan & South India

BOOKS

APPASWAMY, JAYA 1044
    'Tanjur Paintings of the Maratha Period'
(Abhinav, New Delhi 1978)

ARAVAMUTHAN, T. G. 1045
    'South Indian Portraits'
(London 1930)

BARRETT, DOUGHLAS 1046
    'Painting of the Deccan XVI-XVII Centuries'
(London 1957)
Reviewed in the LK No. 7 (April 1960) 106-8

KRAMRISCH, STELLA 1047
    'Survey of Painting in the Deccan'
(London 1937)
Mural paintings of Ajanta Ellora and Vijaynagar; also deals with Deccani
miniatures

MITTAL, JAGDISH 1048
    'Andhra Painting of the Ramayana'
(Hyderabad 1969) 63 pls (10 colour)
From the Rāmāyaṇa ms. of mid-18th century at Hyderabad

ARTICLES

ANAND, M. R. (ed.) 1049
'Glass Paintings of Hyderabad' &
'Deccani Paintings…… '
Marg XVI-2 (March 1963) 57-64, 15 pls

ASHRAF, M., SKELTON, R. & OTHERS 1050
'(Paintings of) Ahmednagar, Bijapur & Golconda'
Marg XVI-2 (March 1963) 25-42, 20 pls (2 colour)

BARRETT, DOUGHLAS 1051
'Some Unpublished Deccan Miniatures'
LK No. 7 (April 1960) 9-13, 7 pls (1 colour)
Deals with a Golconda set of 1586-90 A. D., Bijapur of 1660 A. D. and other
miniatures

BAWA, V. K. & MOHIUDDIN, SYED 1052
'Rulers of the Centres of Deccani Painting'
Marg XVI-2 (March 1963) Supp. pages (i) to (x)

BUKHARI, Y. K. 1053
'An Unpublished Illuminated Manuscript entitled
Fawāid-i-Quṭb Shāhī'
LK No. 13 (1967) 9-10, 3 pls (1 colour)

CHAGHTAI, M. A. 1054
'A Treasury of Biographical Sketches of Great Men'
Isc IX-3 (July 1935)

GOETZ, H. 1055
'Notes on a Collection of Historical Portraits from Golconda'
IAL X-1 (1936) 10-21, 2 pls

GOETZ, H. 1056
'(A) Unique Deccani Miniature'
BMB I-1 (Aug 1943-Jan 1944) 37-42

GOSWAMY, B. N.   1057
  'Deccani Painting'
LK No. 12 (Oct 1962) 41–44
An opinion on an Illustrated ms. in the British Museum, critique of D. Barrett's
'Some Unpublished Deccan Miniatures' LK 7 (April 1960) 9-13

JOSHI, P. M.   1058
  'Ibrahim Adil Shah II of Bijapur'
March of India VII-2 (1954) 17–19
Illustrations of His painting and a page from his **Kitāb-i-Nauras**

KHANDALAVALA, KARL J.   1059
  'Reflections on Deccani Painting'
Marg XVI-2 (March 1963) 23-24

KRAMRISCH, STELLA   1060
  'Daksina-Chitra'
JISOA V (1937) 218-37
On Deccanese Painting

MITTAL, JAGDISH   1061
  'Deccani Painting : Golconda & Hyderabad School'
Dr G. Yazdani Com. Vol. (Hyderabad 1966) 127-33, 5 pls

MITTAL, JAGDISH   1062
  'Paintings of the Hyderabad School'
Marg XVI-2 (March 1963) 43-56, 28 pls

MITTAL, JAGDISH   1063
  'Some Deccani Paintings in the Baroda Museum'
BMB XX (1968) 19-25 and 13 pls

MITTAL, JAGDISH; WELCH, S. C. & ETTINGHAUSEN, R.   1064
  'Portfolio (of Deccani Paintings)'
Marg XVI-2 (March 1963) 7-22, 32 pls (1 colour)
Excellent visuals

MOTICHANDRA   1065
  'Dakhini Kalam - Bijapur'
Kala-Nidhi Banares I-1
On Bijapur paintings of the late 16th and early 17th century A. D.

MOTICHANDRA 1066
    'Portraits of Ibrahim Adil Shah II'
Marg V-1 (Dec 1951) 22-28, 6 pls
Bijapur school

MOTICHANDRA & KHANDALAVALA, KARL J. 1067
    'Identification of the Portraits of Malik Ambar'
LK 1-2 (April 1955-March 1956) 23-31, 5 pls (1 colour)

NAZIR AHMED 1068
    'Farukh Husain, the Royal Artist at the Court of Ibrahim
    'Adil Shah II & His Painting'
IsC XXX-1 (Jan 1956) ; *also published in the AIOC XVII (1953)
395-400*

NAZIR AHMED 1069
    'Shāh Khalīlullah Khushnawīs, the Royal Calligraphist
    of the Adil Shahi Court'
IsC XLIV-1 (Jan 1970) 35-55
A detailed survey of his life and work.

SKELTON, R. 1070
    'Documents for the Study of Painting at Bijapur in the late
    16th and early 17th centuries'
Arts Asiatiques V (1958) 97-125, 6 illus

SRINIVASAN, K. R. 1071
    'South Indian Paintings'
PIHC (1944) 168-76

YAZDANI, G. 1072
    'Two Miniatures from Bijapur'
IsC IX-2 (April 1935)

6

RAGA-MALA PAINTING
(Mughal, Rajput, Pahari & Deccani)

BOOKS

DAHMEN-DALLAPICCOLA, A. L. 1073
'Raga Mala-Miniaturen' (1475–1700 A. D.)
(Wiesbaden 1975) Text in German, plates in English
Rāgamālā miniatures from 18 sets; a very standard work

EBELING, KLAUS 1074
'Ragamala Painting'
(Paris, New Delhi 1973)
The most authoritative work on the Raga Mala Painting; reviewed by Khandalavala in the LK No. 19 (1979) 63-65

GANGOLY, O. C. 1075
'Ragas & Raginis'
Vol. I Text (Nalanda Pub. Bombay 1948);
Vol. II (Calcutta 1955) with pls
A pictorial and Iconographic Study of Indian Musical modes based on original sources; a very learned and authoritative work

KHANDALAVALA, KARL J. (ed.) 1076
'Ragamala Paintings'
(Portfolio of the Lalit Kala Akademi New Delhi 1968)

NAWAB, VIDYA SARABHAI   1077
'419 Illustrations of Indian Music and Dance in Western
Indian Style'
(*Ahmedabad 1964*)
An excellent catalogue of 15th-16th century miniatures with 4 colour and 419
monotone pls

PAL, P.   1078
'Raga–Mala Paintings in the Museum of Fine Arts Boston'
(*Boston 1967*)

RANDHAWA, M. S.   1079
'Kangra Ragamala Paintings'
(*National Museum New Delhi 1971*) *pp. 88, 99 pls (20 colour)*
On the classical theme of Rāga-Rāginīs in the Kangra series, reviewed in the LK
No. 18, 47-48

SATYA PRAKASH   1080
'Raga–Ragini Miniatures from the Central Museum Jaipur'
(*Jaipur 1960*)
Brief introduction and 36 exquisite colour pls of Rāga-Rāginī miniatures of late
17th or early 18th century Jaipur style

STOOKE, H. J. & KHANDALAVALA, KARL J.   1081
'(The) Laud Raga Mala Miniatures'
(*London 1953*)

WALDSHMIDT, ERNST & ROSE LEONORE   1082
'Miniatures of Musical Inspiration'
Part—I
(*Bombay 1967*)
On the Iconography of the Raga Mala paintings; reviewed by Khandalavala in
the LK No. 15 (1972) 66-67; D. Barrett's letter in this connection in LK No. 17,
p. 58

ARTICLES

ANDHARE, SHRIDHAR   1083
'(A) Dated Amber Ragamala and the Problem of Provenance
of the 18th century Jaipuri Paintings'
LK No. 15 (1972) 47-51, 13 pls
A set of 32 paintings done in 1709 A. D. preserved at Kankroli; a very interesting
article

ANDHARE, SHRIDHAR   1084
'(An) Early Ragamala from the Kankroli Collection'
BPOW No. 12 (1973) 58-64, 12 pls
C. 1590-1600 A. D.

BAHURA, G. N. & CHANDRAMANI SINGH   1085
'Some Illustrated Rajasthani Manuscripts'
(from the Maharaja Sawai Mansingh II Museum Jaipur)
Art Heritage No. 2 (n. d.) 39-54
15 pls on Rāga-Mālā and Krishṇa-Rukmiṇī-rī-Bel of early 17th century painted
at Agra/Delhi; Bihārī-Satsaī and Nāyikā-Bheda of 17th century and other miniatures and wooden covers of 18th century; a very interesting and useful study

BANERJI, ADRIS   1086
'Malwa School of Painting'
Roop-Lekha XXXI-1 (June 1960) 32-42, 6 pls
Late 17th century Rāga Mālā paintings of Narsinghgarh

BROWN, W. NORMAN   1087
'Some Early Rajasthani Raga Paintings'
JISOA XVI (1948) 1-10

EBELING, KLAUS   1088
'Confusing Iconographies in Rajput Ragamalas'
BMB XXIII (1971) 35-70, 44 pls
Almost a monograph indispensable for the study of Rāgamālā paintings

GANGOLY, O. C.   1089
'New Acquisitions of Ragini Miniatures'
BMB XIX (1966) 29-31

GOETZ, H.   1090
'(The) Laud Ragamala Album and Early Rajput Painting'
Journal of Royal Asiatic Society London I (1954) 63-74 & 4 pls

KANORIA, G. K.   1091
'An Early Dated Rajasthani Raga-Mala'
JISOA XIX (1952-53) 1-10 and pls

KHANDALAVALA, KARL J.   1092
'(The) Laud Raga Mala Miniatures'
Marg VI-4 (Dipawali 1953) 26-29, 6 pls (3 colour)
A very learned and useful article

MEHTA, N. C.   1093
    'A Note on Ragamala'
JISOA III (1935) 145-47

MUKHERJEE, HIREN   1094
    'Two Early Rajasthani Ragini Pictures'
LK No. 12 (Oct 1962) 39-40, 2 pls
Of Mewar, c. 1600 A. D.

PARIMOO, RATAN   1094-A
    'Dated Ragamala from Radhanpur'
    (Mesakarna and Muftahusarur)
JOI XXX. 3-4 (March-June 1981) 231-50, 16 pls
Ms. of 84 'musical' paintings dated 1896/1839 from Gujarat

PRAMOD CHANDRA   1095
    'A Ragamala Set of the Mewar School in the National
    Museum'
LK Nos. 3-4 (April 1956-March 1957) 46-54 and pls

RANDLE, H. N.   1096
    'A Note on the India Office Raga Mala Collection'
New Indian Antiquary IV (1941) 162-73

RASIKA   1097
    'Ragamala Paintings from Rajasthan'
Marg XI-2 (March 1958) 25-29, 7 pls

SAGATSINGH   1098
    'Rajasthani Chitrakala men Ragon ka Svarupa' (Hindi)'
RB XI. 1-4 (1969) 147-62
On the Rāgamālā paintings set preserved in the Government Museum Bikaner

SANGRAM SINGH, KUMAR   1099
    'An Early Ragamala Ms. from Pali (Marwar School)
    dated 1623 A. D.'
LK No. 7 (April 1960) 9 pls (1 colour)

SASTRY, B. V. K.   1100
    'Musical Iconography in Shri Tatva-Nidhi'
QJNCPA IV-1 (March 1975) 8-19
On Rāga-Mālā Paintings

SHAH, U. P. 1101
    'Three Paintings from a New Ragamala set dated Samvat
       1665 (= 1608-9 A.D.)'
BMB XXV (1973 74) 89-94, 3 pls

SHASTRI, HIRANANDA 1102
    'Were Ragamalas Painted by the Artists of Kangra ?'
JBORS XVII (1931) 101-3

VIJAY KRISHNA 1103
    'Fantasy in Indian Art'
CHHAVI I (1971) 335-38, 18 pls (1 colour)
Alludes to the fantasy in Rāgamalā paintings

7

COMPANY & BENGALI PAINTING
(19th—20th Centuries)

BOOKS

APPASAMY, JAYA   1104
'Abanindranath Tagore and the Art of his Times'
(*Lalit Kala Akademi New Delhi 1968*) *pp. 142, 44 pls*

APPASAMY, JAYA (ed.)   1105
'Portfolio of Contemporary Paintings'
(*Lalit Kala Akademi, New Delhi 1969*)

APPASAMY, JAYA & OTHERS   1106
'Twentyfive Years of Indian Art'
(Painting Sculpture and Graphics in the Post-Independence
Era)
(*Lalit Kala Akademi New Delhi 1973*) *pp. 32, 32 pls (6 colour)*
On Modern Indian Art and Artists; good appraisal

ARCHER, MILDRED   1107
'British Drawings in the Indian Office Library'
2 vols
(*London 1969*) *122 pls (2 colour)*
A grand catalogue of 10,976 drawings by British Artists of 18th and 19 centuries

ARCHER, MILDRED   1108
'Company Drawings in the India Office Library'
(*London 1972*)
On the paintings of the Company's period

ARCHER, MILDRED   **1109**
'Indian Popular Paintings in the India Office Library'
(*London 1977*) *pp. 196, 92 pls*

ARCHER, MILDRED   **1110**
'Natural History Drawings in the Indian Office Library'
(*London 1962*)
On the paintings of the Company period; reviewed in the LK No.10
(Oct 1961) p.65

ARCHER, MILDRED   **1111**
'Patna Painting'
(*London 1947*)
Of Company School

ARCHER, MILDRED & W. G.   **1112**
'Indian Painting for the British 1770-1880'
(*London 1955*)
Of Company School

ARCHER, W. G.   **1113**
'Kalighat Drawings'
(*Marg Publications Bombay 1962*)
19th and 20th century drawings for popular consumption

ARCHER, W. G.   **1114**
'Kalighat Paintings'
(*Victoria & Albert Museum London 1971*)
On the so-called Bazar Paintings of Calcutta from 1800 to 1930 A. D. made by
village artists for sale to the pilgrims who came to the Kalighat Temple

CHANDRA, R. G.   **1115**
'Abanindranath Tagore'
(*Calcutta 1951*) *pp. 104, 41 illus.*

DUTTA, A. K.   **1116**
'Jamini Roy'
(*Lalit Kala Akademi New Delhi 1973 Contemporary Art Series*) *pp. 40*

GANGOLY, O. C.   **1117**
'Modern Indian Artists'
2 vols
(*Calcutta 1923*)

NEOGY, P.   1118
'Drawings and Paintings of Rabindranath Tagore'
(*Lalit Kala Akademi New Delhi 1961*) *with 40 colour pls*

PARIMOO, RATAN   1119
'Paintings of Three Tagores : Abanindranath, Gaganendranath
and Rabindranath'
(Chronology and Comparative Study)
(*Baroda 1973*) *pp. viii + 182 with 9 figs and 387 pls*

RAMACHANDRA RAO, P. R.   1120
'Modern Indian Painting'
(*Madras*)
A masterpiece on contemporary Indian Art

ARTICLES

APPASAMY, JAYA   1121
'Artists of the Bengal School and that Period'
Lalit Kala Contemporary No. 1 (New Delhi)

APPASAMY, JAYA   1122
'Ksitindranath Majumdar'
CHHAVI I (1971) 218-23 with pls

ARCHER, MILDRED   1123
'James Wales : Portrait Painter in Bombay and Poona
1791-95'
JISOA New Series VIII (1976-77) 57-64

ARCHER, MILDRED   1124
'Notes on Painting' and 'Bazaar Style'
Marg XX-1 (Dec 1966) 46-54, 26 pls

ARCHER, W. G.   1125
'Banares and British Art'
CHHAVI I (1971) 43-47 with pls
18th-19th century Company Art

ARCHER, W. G.   1126
    'Kalighat Painting'
Marg V-4 (Sept 1952) 22-28, 10 pls
Popular Art of Bengal

ARCHER, W. G.   1127
    'Maithil Painting'
Marg III-3 (April 1949) 24-33, 10 pls
Mainly wall paintings in Modern times

CHAKRABORTI, JAYANTA   1128
    'Kalighat Painting'
*Bulletin of School of Oriental and African Studies London XXVIII-3
(1975) 57-63*

CHATTERJI, KEDARNATH   1129
    'Modern Bengali Painting'
JISOA I (1933) 89-96

CHATTERJI, S. K.   1130
    'Abanindranath : Master-Artist and Renovator in Art'
JISOA Golden Jubilee Number (1961) 54-65
A learned treatise on a great artist

COUSINS, JAMES H.   1131
    '(The) Art of Asit Kumar Haldar'
RUPAM No. 9 (Jan 1922) 1-4

DAS, S. R.   1132
    '(A) Note on Domestic Painting of Bengal-Alpana'
Proceedings of Indian Science Congress Baroda 1955 Vol. XLII, 324

KRISHNAN, S. A.   1133
    'Ramkinkar Baij'
LK Nos. 1-2 (April 1955-March 1956) 94-95, 4 pls
Introducing the great Painter & Sculptor of Shanti-Niketan

MITRA, S. C.   1134
    'Bengal School of Art'
AIOC III (1924) 74-75

MITRA, S. C.   **1135**
    'Bengal School of Art (Origin & Varieties of Indian Art)'
IHQ I 1-2 (1925) 69-79, 303-9

PARIMOO, RATAN   **1136**
    '(The) Chronology of the Paintings of Gaganendranath
      Tagore'
CHHAVI I (1971) 202-17 with pls

RANDHAWA, M. S.   **1137**
    'Two Panjabi Artists of the Nineteenth Century :
    Kehar Singh and Kapur Singh'
CHHAVI I (1971) 67-69 with pls
On Company Art

RAY CHOWDHURY, D. P.   **1138**
    'Abanindranath & The Bengal School of Painting'
IMB V-2 (July 1970) 9-11

RAY, NIHAR RANJAN   **1139**
    '(The) Bengal School of Painting Today'
JISOA IV (1936) 126-29

SARKAR, BENOY KUMAR   **1140**
    'Tendencies of Modern Indian Art'
RUPAM No. 26 (April 1926) 55-57

SEN, PULINBIHARI   **1141**
    'Works of Abanindranath Tagore : A Bibliography'
JISOA Golden Jubilee Number (1961) 110-13

SUHRAWARDY, SHAHID   **1142**
    '(Art of) Jamini Roy'
Marg II-1 (Oct 1947) 65-77, 18 pls

VAN-GEYZEL, L. C.   **1143**
    '(The) Painting of George Keyt'
Marg I-3 (April 1947) 41-65, 26 pls
Ceylonese painter of the early 20th century

VENKATACHALAM, G.   **1144**
    'Nandlal Bose'
LK Nos. 1-2 (April 1955-March 1956) 90-93, 3 pls (1 colour)
On the Art of the world-renowned Artist of Shanti-Niketan

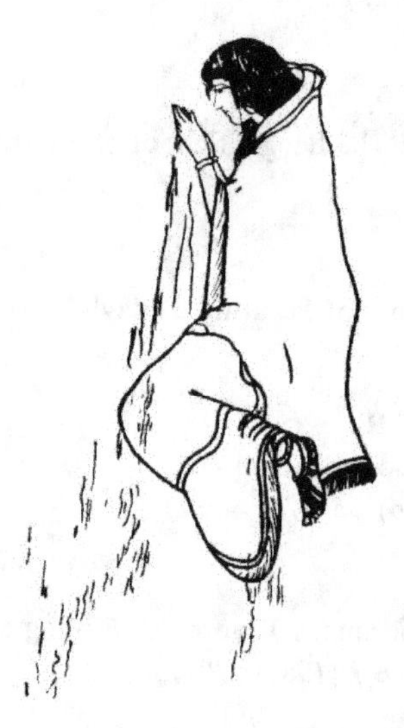

INDICES

INDEX-I

Index to the Titles of Ancient & Medieval Illustrated Works

Index to the Names of Places (in the Titles of Books & Articles)

INDEX-III

Index to Historical Names of Painters & Princes
(in the Titles of Books & Articles)

INDEX-IV

Index to the Titles of Texts (Theories)

INDEX-V

Index to Various Collections of Paintings, Painted Textiles etc.
(in the Titles of Books & Articles)

INDEX-VI

Index to the Names of Modern Authors